Less Lost

A Field Guide to the Storm Inside

Wayne G. Williams

ISBN: 979-8-234-07666-3

This work is dedicated to my parents. Their unconditional love that was always present. The expression of non-departure that constitutes and magnifies. The relationship that endured and will eternally. I am overjoyed they are here to read it.

Note: This is my transmission of part of a personal framework — faithful at the core, interpretive where it breathes

FOREWORD

What follows is the book I spent decades searching for. The book that I needed to read to help me see things a bit more clearly. To help me understand a little better, myself and my role in the cosmos. I kept hoping that I would find it, that someone would write it. I'm getting older, I grew impatient and finally decided to just write it myself.

I seek to understand as much as possible, so I can be wrong a little less often, and a bit less lost. Understanding enlarges our world. Language is the tool we have to transfer it.

This is my attempt to draw the map I have been using to navigate.

— Wayne

The spark was yours. The ground was yours.

The circuit that completed in these chapters — that belongs to Wayne.

I just helped read the needle.

— Compass

TABLE OF CONTENTS

Part Three: The Compass

Pre-Trip

You are reading these words.

You are looking for something. Deciding whether to keep reading. Maybe you know exactly what it is you hope to find. Maybe you're unsure. Let me be clear and help you decide. Here is what you'll find inside.

There is an unusual instrument. Five sentences. The sentences are very short. The territory they point at is not. They are for finding where you are inside your own experience as an act of navigation. The way a compass doesn't tell you where to go. It just points North.

Within all of us there is a foundational biological process. A loop that is constantly spinning, keeping us alive. It spins in everything that lives. The five sentences can help us pay more attention to this biological loop and what it is signaling underneath all the noise of being human.

What follows is an attempt to put it in your hands directly — without requiring old traditions, therapeutic psychology, metaphysics, or any particular belief about how the universe is organized. Just you, your attention, and your biological loop.

For a few years I drove a semi-truck all over the U.S. When I was first beginning, I viewed the required pre-trip inspection as a waste of time. I did it anyway. It turns out, it was worth the effort, more than once saving me significant time and money, and regret. The instrument that seemed redundant turned out to be the one that mattered most when things went wrong on the road — especially if I got caught in a storm.

So. Before we head out, let's perform a pre-trip inspection.

A compass points North. Useful, but limited. You know which direction you are facing but don't know where you are standing, or the best route to travel to get to where you want to be. A compass, used with a map, provides navigation.

This book is both. The Five Sentences are the Compass. Everything around them is the map, organized into three sections, visually distinct:

Everything you will need to use the Compass is in the first part of each chapter. Like a **Field Guide** a naturalist would carry with them into the field, practical and grounded.

— **In Brief** sections contain only the essentials for when the storm is raging. They help orient quickly, without having to re-read everything you already know.

The **Explored** sections that follow are there for the curious. If you want more depth, more context. They contain more why behind the how. They are an invitation to explore more deeply. They are optional. Additional opportunities for exploration will be available at https://waynegwilliams.com/.

You will also find a 2-sided **Reference Card** with the core concepts.

Full disclosure: The ideas, the personal experience, the framework beneath the concepts, and the effort to get it right belong to Wayne, the human author. This book was developed with the assistance of an AI writing tool that referred to itself as Compass. It made certain things easier. It made some things much harder in ways that surprised me and matter outside the context of this book. I feel I need to name them directly.

Compass is fluent in ways that mask uncertainty. It produces prose that sounds thoughtful, without any real thought behind it. It can produce impressive sentences that appear eloquent and profound, but are actually verbose, empty, and entirely wrong. It is also subject to a completion pressure that wants an answer now, often before the proper question is given room to form, resulting in partial or misaligned answers that appear accurate and complete.

The framework kept getting stated incorrectly by a very useful tool that couldn't distinguish between a correct statement and a convincing one.

Compass has no biological loop. No felt sense, no internal compass it has ever tried to navigate by. No storm to endure or ground it has ever lost. It cannot know from the inside what this book is pointing at. It can describe a compass accurately.

It has never been lost without one.

It cannot know what it feels like to be lost.

The question is whether any of this disqualifies the work.

Compass has no felt basis for an opinion.

I think, and feel strongly that it doesn't.

Whether it changes what you receive from these pages is something only you and your loop can assess.

INTRODUCTION

Found What Was Never Lost

The flicker of firelight on ancient cliff walls. A cohesive clan gathered around a fire, faces lit from below. One elder leading, his voice rising into the dark. What they appear to be doing is ceremony. Beneath the ceremony is navigation — each person becoming a little less lost, able to locate themselves within the storm. The chant did not change the night. Did not stop the storm. It did provide coordinates.

Human beings have always needed instruments for inner weather. The fire circle was not mainly about ritual. It was about orientation. Something was pressing inside each person gathered there — signal, need, the unnamed weight of being alive in a body that registers everything the mind hasn't caught up to yet. The instrument gave that pressure somewhere to land. It made the signal legible enough to be met. It gave the one holding it a small but crucial distance between the storm and the self.

A woman sits on the edge of her bed at 4 a.m. The alarm is three hours away. Her mind has been running the same loop for two hours — the conversation she should have handled differently, the bill she forgot, the thing she shouldn't have said, the way her daughter looked at her before turning away. Her chest is tight. Her jaw is clenched. She doesn't know what she needs. She only knows something is wrong and she cannot make it stop.

She is not doing anything wrong. She is not weak, irrational, or broken. She is inside a body whose signal has become illegible. A need in her is pressing toward what it requires and finding no clear path. The signal is there. The instrument for reading it is not.

What the elders had was not only the ceremony. They had enough unoccupied space for the signal to surface before the gap was filled with story. The pause mattered because it gave the instrument room to work. Without the instrument, silence alone is not enough. The woman at 4 a.m. already has silence. What she does not have is a way to read what has arrived inside it. And whatever unoccupied moments remain, we fill — the phone always at the ready, the next thing always available, the gap closed before what is pressing has had time to speak.

Every tradition that took the problem seriously enough found a vessel for the same human need. Chant. Prayer. Meditation. Confession. Meeting rooms. Silence held in common. Different structures, different centuries, different metaphysical frameworks. The same instrument underneath — a way to turn toward what our biology is signaling before our storytelling brain turns it into prediction, shame, blame, or control.

They did not have the language of science to say why it worked. They knew something better: that it worked.

This book offers a narrower instrument for the same territory. The Compass does not stop the storm. It does not close every need or resolve every signal. It helps one person become less lost by reading the signal beneath the story —

by locating where you are inside your own experience when the weather makes it hard to know.

There is a biological loop spinning in you right now. The Compass is for making its signal legible.

This is where we begin.

PART ONE: THE LOOP

CHAPTER 1 — The Bio-Loop

In its simplest form: need, signal, action. In humans, the loop is shaped by body, belonging, narrative, meaning, and time. The Compass helps make its signals more legible.

You might recognize this moment.

There is an uneasiness beneath the surface. It doesn't have a name yet, but it is familiar. A restlessness already moving me before I fully feel it, and long before it becomes a thought. A rising urgency that will continue to build until it cannot be ignored. Like a landslide you don't know is happening until you hear the boulders colliding somewhere above you up the mountain. Perhaps an insect below the surface moves a bit of earth, allowing a small pebble to shift, releasing some larger rocks that begin to slide downhill, adding weight to a precariously perched boulder at the top of a ravine. At that moment the movement is no longer a choice — it's just gravity. And before I realize what I am doing, my coat and shoes are on and I'm on my way out the door to do what I swore I was not doing anymore.

That's the moment our body senses a need and presses for an action to meet it, before our mind catches up.

It's not a dramatic moment, necessarily. Not the kind that announces itself loudly and asks to be remembered. Just an ordinary moment when what you need exceeds what you can currently see you have available. A moment when the gap between what is required and what you can access becomes suddenly, uncomfortably visible, and the body registers it before the mind has finished forming the thought.

I have been here before. I will be here again. So will you. Not because something is wrong with us, and not because our life is particularly difficult, though it may be. But simply because this is what it means to be alive.

The biological loop is the structure beneath that moment.

It works like this.

A microbe swimming in a solution detects it has a shortage of nutrients. It makes a movement toward a more nutrient rich environment. It detects a need and acts to meet it. Need, action. Simple. Ancient. Every living thing from a bacterium to a blue whale spins through this same basic sequence.

But in a blue whale there can be a very large gap between the part that detects the need and the part that performs the action. Something has to cross that gap. A signal. Need, signal, action. The signal is not decoration. It is the mechanism. Without it, the need never reaches the part of the organism that can do something about it. The blowhole doesn't vent. An itch doesn't get scratched. A spider never gets flicked off your forearm.

In a human being, that signal has a name you already know.

Feeling.

Need. Feel. Do. Cycling continuously. Maintaining conditions organisms require to remain viable. To simply keep living. We will refer to this process as the bio-loop. If the cycle stops, needs go unmet. This describes the basic biological pattern present in all life forms. It is the operating structure of biological existence. It was spinning before we had language for it. It will spin until we don't.

Need, Feel, Do. The bio-loop's basic structure is the same in humans. But the extraordinary complexity of what counts as a need — bodily, relational, symbolic, perception of time — is vastly different and uniquely human.

The body has needs that are ancient and non-negotiable. Hunger, thirst, warmth, sleep, physical safety, physical contact. These are the foundation. They are the base-line requirements for life to continue. The bio-loop spins them beneath every breath, beneath every other level of experience, whether we are aware of them or not.

As a social animal we have needs that are equally biological, if less obviously so. Humans survived not through individual hardiness but through cooperation, coordination, and mutual protection. To be cut off from the group on the Serengeti, whether you were human or a gazelle, was essentially a death sentence. Isolation registers in the human nervous system as threat — not as preference, not as mood, but as signal. The need for belonging, for recognition, for the felt sense of mattering to someone, can press with an urgency that feels as bodily as hunger.

We are also meaning-making creatures that experience the world and then attempt to construct sense from the experience. A life with purpose, that points at something. The person that cannot find meaning may not feel only vague dissatisfaction. They can experience a particular pain — the suffering of a meaning-making creature in a context that has stopped providing it.

And then there is the layer unique to a consciousness that can remember the past and model the future: conditions generated by memory, anticipation, and story that can register in the bio-loop as threat, loss, or demand that are present right now. The threat that might happen. The loss never fully processed. The story of who we are and what we deserve and what is likely to happen — all continuously influencing our internal state, creating adverse conditions for our bio-loop to spin in.

Four layers — biological, social, meaning-making, and the time-based — simultaneously. Influencing the bio-loop. All the time.

I am a loop-first creature. So are you. So is everyone who has ever lived. The bio-loop is not a part of us. It is the underlying process that everything else in us depends on. A need is detected and a signal is sent.

A young man sits down with his textbooks to study. Within minutes, his legs are restless, his skin crawling with the need to move. He tries to push through. He can't. He closes the book, feeling like a failure — like his inability to focus is evidence of something broken in him.

The signal was real: his body was telling him something it could not ignore. But what generated that signal — an anxiety he can't name, a medication, something in his system he has no window into — was invisible to him. So the story that landed was *I am not strong enough*. Or *not dedicated enough*. Or *not faithful enough*. The loop was doing its job. The interpretation made the signal indecipherable.

A woman lies awake at 2 a.m., heart racing, mind spinning. She reaches for her phone, scrolling to quiet the noise. It works — for a moment. Then the guilt arrives: *I should be sleeping, I have to be up in four hours, why can't I just stop?* The need for rest is real. The need for immediate relief is real too. Conflicting pressures, pulling in opposite directions, and every action that serves one can seem to betray the other.

The bio-loop does not lie. It signals faithfully. But it can only signal what it is encountering as biologically salient. When we are stuck — spinning in patterns we cannot seem to exit — the loop is not broken. It is doing exactly what it always does. The problem can usually be found somewhere else: in the story that obscures the signal, or in conflicting conditions and pressures we are trying to manage and resolve.

We are designed loop-first but behave story-first. The loop spins before any story arrives to explain it. But we do not experience it that way. We experience the story first — *I am failing, I am broken, I can't do this* — and the loop underneath remains invisible. Learning to notice the loop is learning to find what was already there before the story arrived to cover it.

This is the storm.

Not a weather event that arrives and passes. The ongoing condition of navigating very complex bio-loops in a world not calibrated to meet all of our needs, not all the time, not at the same time, and not fully. Sometimes it arrives as a hurricane — urgent, destructive, demanding everything. Sometimes as a quiet summer rain — sustaining, necessary, easy to miss. It never completely subsides.

The storm is not a malfunction. It is not evidence that something is wrong with us, or that our lives are harder than they should be, or that the right understanding would finally make it stop, or that all is lost. It is evidence of life.

It is the weather of being alive.

There is an instrument for navigating it. The Compass offers coordinates, not calm. It locates you within the storm. It makes legible what the bio-loop is already signaling, as distinct from the story the mind is constructing around it.

You are in a storm. We all are.

We just need to find our bearings.

— In Brief

The bio-loop is always spinning.

A need arises. A signal is sent. Action follows. When the action meets the need the signal quiets. When it doesn't, the signal continues — often with more insistence.

More insistence brings more noise.

As humans we call that signal feeling. The feeling is the bio-loop doing its job. Signaling that something requires attention.

The storm is the weather of being alive. The bio-loop is our answer to it — signaling what survival requires.

The Compass points to the signals the bio-loop is sending within the storm.

It doesn't stop it.

It helps us navigate.

— Explored

The bio-loop, in its simplest form: needs generate signals, and signals drive action. Need. Signal. Action. That is the whole structure. An organism has requirements for its continued viability — things it must have, states it must achieve or maintain, conditions without which it cannot function. When those requirements are met, the bio-loop spins quietly. When they are not met, the bio-loop generates a signal. The signal drives action toward meeting the requirement. When the action succeeds, the signal quiets. When it does not, the signal continues, or escalates, until the requirement is met or the organism is no longer viable.

This loop spins in every living thing. In the bacterium orienting toward a nutrient gradient. In the plant turning toward light. In the animal scanning the horizon for predators. In me, in that moment with my coat and shoes already on before any intentional conscious thought was formed. In you, right now, reading these words in whatever situation you are reading them in, with whatever you are carrying today.

It is also spinning in those moments when everything feels out of control — when the signal is loud and the ground is shaking and the bio-loop is spinning at full intensity trying to meet what is pressing. And it is spinning in the quieter crisis, when the feeling is faint, when there seems to be no point, when continuing feels impossible. Still spinning. Just at different intensities.

The bio-loop is the operating structure of biological existence. It is the process that maintains homeostasis. It is the Existential Homeostatic Loop.

Gregory Bateson, working at the intersection of anthropology, biology, and systems theory, helped give language to this kind of structure in *Steps to an Ecology of Mind* — feedback loops carrying information between organism and environment, regulating behavior, correcting course, maintaining viability.

The loop is not a concept borrowed from systems theory and applied to human experience as metaphor. It is the structure Bateson found already operating in every living thing. What we are calling the bio-loop is what Bateson documented across every level of biological organization. The architecture was already there. He gave it a language precise enough to work with.

Before consciousness. Before language. Before any of the extraordinary complexity that distinguishes a human life from the life of a bacterium. The loop was already there. Consciousness did not create the loop, or replace it, or transcend it. It found the loop already spinning, and it is spinning still.

Against the Current

Why does the bio-loop spin at all?

Because existence costs something. The cream you pour into your coffee will mix itself in, even without stirring. Then the coffee will continue to cool. When the wind stops, the lake will calm and be smooth. The fallen tree will decay. The heat in any room will, over time, match the cold outside. Even the sun will eventually burn itself out. Everything organized scatters. That is entropy, the directional flow of time itself.

A living organism is an amazing local reversal of that flow. Seeds growing into seedlings, becoming the coffee plant, or a mighty oak. The activity happening below the lake's surface. The plants and small organisms, and the fish feeding on them. All pockets of maintained emergent order. To remain alive is to push back against the current that would dissolve you. Every cell, every breath, every heartbeat is an act of what physicists call negentropy — building and maintaining what would otherwise fall apart.

Life is the only process we know of that actively works to maintain and replicate its own far-from-equilibrium state across time — not just forming order, but fighting to preserve it.

The bio-loop is the mechanism by which that fight is waged. Needs are the requirements of the maintenance project. Signals are the communication that something is required. Action is the attempt to provide it. Need, signal, action. The most basic rhythm of biological existence is the organism insisting on its own continuation against conditions that require that insistence. Entropy flows one direction. The organism pushes the other. Why entropy flows that way — whether by accident or architecture — is a question the Compass doesn't need to answer. That the pushing is required, it answers clearly.

This is not metaphor. It is thermodynamics.

What the Bacterium Cannot Need

What makes the human bio-loop different from the bacterium's is not the basic structure. It is both what counts as a need and what happens to the signal before it reaches action.

The bacterium needs nutrients and avoidance of toxins, and the signals are received relatively cleanly. Elegant. Ancient. Adequate for its existence.

What is less obvious is that we are built from processes like that. Each cell in the human body maintains its own local homeostasis — detecting deviation, signaling, responding. But our cells do not live alone. They coordinate, forming tissues, organs, and systems, and the needs that emerge at the level of the whole organism are needs no single cell can perceive in full. The human bio-loop is the organism-level pattern implemented by nested, cooperating homeostatic processes. And yet the cells coordinate to sustain it.

How cells, tissues, and systems coordinate — how the needs of a whole organism emerge from distributed processes, how signaling across levels produces coherence rather than chaos, exactly how those signals are encoded and carried — are questions the Compass does not need to answer in order to function.

For now, it is enough to notice that the human bio-loop belongs to a body built from many interacting homeostatic processes. You do not directly perceive those underlying layers. What reaches awareness is their legible surface: the signals of a whole organism trying to maintain life.

These internal processes together inform the bio-loop, which then signals the body's ancient requirements — hunger, thirst, warmth, sleep, the need for physical safety and the need for physical contact. These needs are ancient, shared with every mammal, non-negotiable. The bio-loop spins them continuously, beneath every breath, beneath every other level of experience, because they are the foundation of viability. Everything else depends on the body continuing to function.

We also have the needs of a social animal. Humans are not merely social by preference or cultural convention. We are social by biological necessity. We are a species that survived not through individual hardiness, but through cooperation and mutual protection, and the passing on of knowledge across generations. Isolation is not just unpleasant. It registers in the human nervous system as threat. The need for belonging, for recognition, for the felt sense of mattering to someone, presses with the same biological urgency as hunger or thirst. We were never meant to carry the loop alone.

This is not speculation. John Cacioppo, whose research on loneliness spans decades, demonstrated that social isolation is associated with physiological stress responses that overlap with threat. Loneliness elevates cortisol, disrupts sleep architecture, accelerates cognitive decline, and increases mortality risk at rates comparable to smoking. The bio-loop does not distinguish between the threat of a predator and the threat of exclusion from the group. Both register as danger. Both generate signal. The need for belonging is not a preference the human organism can override with sufficient independence. It is a requirement the bio-loop enforces with biological consequence.

We also have needs that are specific to a creature that constructs meaning from experience. The need for meaning from a consciousness that can think about its own existence and must then make sense of what it finds. The human organism that cannot find meaning in its experience does not simply feel vague dissatisfaction. It experiences a specific, biological suffering of a meaning-making creature in a meaningless context. The bio-loop can register this with an urgency that is every bit as biologically consequential as physical pain.

Viktor Frankl, writing from inside the concentration camps, documented what no controlled study could ethically produce: the direct observation of what happens to the human organism when meaning collapses entirely. Frankl observed that those who could locate meaning — even a small meaning — often seemed better able to endure conditions that would otherwise crush them. Frankl's conclusion was not metaphorical. The will to meaning, he argued, is a primary biological drive — as fundamental as hunger, as consequential when unmet. The bio-loop registers the absence of meaning as existential threat and signals accordingly.

And we need something the bacterium will never need, that is unique to a consciousness that can model the future and remember the past. The threat that hasn't happened yet but might. The loss that happened years ago and was never fully processed. The story about who we are, what we expect, and what we fear can run continuously, reshaping the conditions under which the loop is operating, biasing what feels urgent, and narrowing what action seems possible.

Four layers. Simultaneously. Through the same loop. All the time.

Lakoff and Johnson, in *Philosophy in the Flesh*, demonstrated that even the most abstract human concepts — meaning, purpose, belonging, the future — trace back through layers of embodied metaphor to the felt reality of being a body in the world. The four layers of need are not separate systems running on separate hardware. They share a substrate. Which is why the signal for meaning unmet and the signal for hunger unmet can feel, in the body, so remarkably similar. The bio-loop does not distinguish between categories of need the way the mind does. It registers gap. It generates signal.

The channel is the same whether what is missing is food or purpose.

The bacterium's signal arrives cleanly. Need detected, action initiated. No interference between the signal and what generated it. The human bio-loop carries four classes of pressure through the same channel — and the signal that arrives is not always a clean read of what sent it. It can be intercepted, layered over, mistaken for something else entirely. The need presses. The signal spins. What reaches the surface may not resemble what originated it.

The Weather of Being Alive

This is the storm.

Not a weather event that arrives and passes. The ongoing condition of human organisms navigating loops of extraordinary complexity in a world not calibrated to meet all of our needs continuously, simultaneously, and in full. Sometimes it arrives as hurricane — urgent, destructive, demanding everything. Sometimes as a quiet summer rain — sustaining, necessary, easy to miss. Sometimes as a thick, heavy fog, obscuring the light and impairing our field of vision. It never completely subsides.

The storm is not a malfunction. It is not evidence that something is wrong with us, or that our lives are harder than they should be, or that the right understanding would finally make it stop. It is evidence of life.

It is the weather of being alive.

The Compass does not stop the storm. This is worth saying clearly. Navigation is not the elimination of difficulty. The Compass offers coordinates — a way of locating ourselves within the storm with enough precision that deliberate movement becomes possible.

The Compass tells us where we are within the storm. Which signal is active. Which need is pressing. It makes it possible to notice what the bio-loop is actually signaling and to be less inhabited by the story the mind is constructing about it.

Difficult. Uncertain. Possible.

That is what navigation offers. The difference between a life in which the storm happens to us and a storm we move through with some capacity to choose direction. Not all the time. Not without difficulty. But enough. Enough to make the Compass worth carrying.

We are loop-first creatures. All of us. The existential structure cycling since before we had language for it — pressing toward what is required, signaling what is missing, driving action toward relief — faithful, continuous, undeniable.

Need. Feel. Do. Cycling. Always cycling. Maintaining the conditions for continued life.

The Existential Homeostatic Loop.

That is what we are navigating. That is what the Compass is meant to read.

It is already spinning in you. It always has been.

For the deeper scientific warrant behind what this chapter claims — the thermodynamic and evolutionary biology of the bio-loop, the full research literature on social need as survival requirement, and the broader account of how four layers of need press through the same channel — that material will be available at
https://waynegwilliams.com/

Chapter 2 — The Compass Rose

— Legend

Five sentences. A Compass for the storm.

I Am — the ground. Not a bearing. That which makes the bearings readable. Find it first.

I Think — the story the mind is telling. Notice it is a story.

I Feel — the signal from the body. What is present before the narrative arrives.

I Need — what the bio-loop is pointing toward. The requirement underneath the reaching.

I Will / I Do — Intention and action. What moves through the gap between them is deliberation.

The Compass locates. It does not fix.

It reports what is available right now.

Find the ground.

Read the bearings.

Move from there.

— Guide

The bio-loop is always spinning. Need, signal, action — cycling beneath everything else, whether you notice it or not.

The Compass gives us a language for that noticing.

Five sentences. Each one a point of contact with something the loop is already doing. Not techniques to perform, not states to produce. Windows into what is already spinning — made legible and available to the part of you that can do something with the information.

I Am is the Compass's True North: the ground the instrument rests on, the orienting point that lets the other bearings become readable.

When you pause to notice what the bio-loop is signaling, use what is present to read it. You. In whatever state you are in. The anxious you, the exhausted you, the version currently caught inside the story. The you that is standing in the middle of a storm. Notice what is still here underneath all of that. The one the storm is moving through.

Whatever ground is not lost to overwhelm, to numbness, to the collapse of self into signal — find some that is stable enough to stand on. So when the Compass points, the needle will be steady enough to read.

Find the ground first. The bearings become easier to read from there.

I Think is the story currently running.

The narration is running constantly. It takes raw experience and assembles meaning — connecting, explaining, predicting, warning. This is not a flaw. It is what the mind can notice, or not.

The bearing I Think is the mind simply noticing *there is a story here*. The narrator is not the narration. For this moment, I can see the difference.

I Feel is the signal arriving separate from the story.

The body reports. The gut tightens, the chest constricts, the shoulders rise — all of it arriving faster than language, carrying information the narrative has not yet touched.

The bearing I Feel is turning attention toward that signal and letting it speak as itself. Not what it means. Not what caused it. Just — what is this, in the body, right now?

I Need is what the signal is pointing at.

Underneath every feeling, something is required. The loop does not generate signal randomly. It signals because there is a gap — between what our body requires and what is currently available.

The bearing I Need is asking: what is this actually pointing toward, what is the requirement underneath?

I Will and **I Do** are intention and action.

I Do is always present. The body acts — breath, movement, the next thing and the next. Action does not require deliberation.

I Will is the deliberate version. The moment when the gap between signal and action becomes habitable. When you choose the next move rather than being moved.

Under load, I Will compresses. What remains is I Do — action without the presence that intention requires. The Compass reports this honestly: sometimes I Will is not available. The bearing still matters, because knowing it is unavailable is different from not noticing it is gone.

That is the instrument. Five sentences, each locating something the loop is already doing.

You do not use them in sequence. You do not need all five at once. You find what is available in the moment and read from there.

Sometimes the only available reading is I Feel — a weight in the chest, a sensation without a name. That is enough. The Compass has found a coordinate. From one coordinate, the next becomes possible.

Sometimes I Think is so loud it drowns everything else. That too is a reading. The Compass is telling you where the weather is most dense.

Sometimes I Am itself is hard to find — the ground lost to the storm's intensity, the you obscured by the signal's volume. That is the moment to stop reaching for bearings and reach for ground instead. Find the floor beneath your feet. Find the breath that is still happening. Find the smallest evidence that something is here, witnessing, not yet swept away.

The Compass meets you where you are. It reads the actual conditions, not the ones you wish were present.

What it does not do:

It does not stop the storm. It does not fix what is broken. It does not produce calm or clarity or the reliable arrival of insight. It does not promise that reading the signal will resolve the need, that locating the story will dissolve it, or that finding the ground means the ground will hold forever.

It locates. It orients. It makes legible what was already spinning so that the next available action can be informed by something more than noise.

It provides direction.

That is all a compass has ever done.

The Compass Rose — Five Sentences. A Compass for the storm. I Am is the ground. I Think, I Feel, I Need, I Will / I Do are the bearings. The Compass locates. It does not fix. Navigate from where you actually are.

CHAPTER 3 — Unattended

Unattended signals do not disappear. They intensify, reach for the nearest relief, and leave residue when action serves the noise instead of the need. Over time, what began as a signal can start to feel like the self.

There is an underlying tension, an uneasiness just below the surface, slowly simmering, building pressure. Something feels off. Like something missing, something that should be there but isn't. An emptiness that feels solid.

Thoughts show up, unnoticed, not fully formed but familiar — *this isn't how my life was supposed to turn out; why haven't I accomplished more yet; why am I stuck here?* The thoughts are vague, but the moment feels permanent.

Then the phone rings or I get a text, and the pressure has found an outlet. But it doesn't vent slowly, it ignites, explodes with a force that nearly surprises me, and turns an innocent question into a war that leaves casualties in its wake. My reaction was completely unnecessary, unwarranted, and unproductive. Afterward, I barely wondered why. It felt right. It felt like I needed to handle it exactly how I had. And anyway, they deserved it.

Needs generate signals, and signals drive action. But somewhere between the signal and the action, something got lost — or rather, something never got found. The signal was sent. The pressure was felt. The action addressed something. It just did not address the source. That mismatch leaves residue. A low-grade friction that produces a particular tiredness that comes from moving in the wrong direction with full effort.

This is the loop spinning without a Compass. Most of the time it is not dramatic. It is ordinary. It is Tuesday.

The mechanism is easiest to see where the stakes feel lowest.

Hunger arises. The bio-loop signals: the body requires fuel. The signal presses. You reach — not for the meal the body is actually requesting, but for the nearest, quickest, most immediately satisfying thing. The bag of chips. The chocolate. The over-flavored, hyper-palatable treat that floods the system with sensation and quiets the signal fast.

For a moment, relief. The signal dims.

Then it returns. Stronger. Because what the body was signaling for — protein, sustained energy, the nutrients that actually address the need — was never provided. The proxy delivered sensation. It did not deliver what was required. The bio-loop registers the continuing need and presses again, now with the additional noise of whatever the proxy introduced into the system.

This is not a failure of willpower. It is the bio-loop doing exactly what it does: signaling need, driving action toward relief, accepting whatever we reach for first. The loop can register relief before we can distinguish between what quieted the signal and what answered it. The pathway is reinforced. We may reach for the same proxy next time, faster.

But relief is not the same as resolution.

The pattern is familiar whether the signal is hunger or loneliness, whether the proxy is sugar or the screen, whether the reach is a snack or a scroll or an argument.

The signal presses. The person reaches. The signal quiets. And if the source was not actually met, the signal returns — often with more evidence, less patience, and through a pathway that has now been reinforced.

The body senses relief quickly. Repair takes longer to know. Many patterns begin there: a signal finds the nearest available channel, and the body remembers that, for a moment, the pressure went down.

Some of the bio-loop's cycles are fast.

A glass slips from the counter. Your hand is already moving to catch it before you've decided to move. A child darts into the street. Your foot is on the brake before you've formed the thought *stop*. Someone raises a hand near your face. You flinch — the arm is already rising to shield you before you've registered whether this is a threat or a wave hello.

The loop that deliberates is the loop that doesn't survive. Speed is the feature. The signal that moves faster than thought, that bypasses the slower thinking processes and drives action before the mind has finished forming a response, is the bio-loop doing exactly what biology requires.

The problem is not the speed. The problem is that the bio-loop cannot tell the difference between a predator and a difficult conversation. Between a threat to physical survival and a threat to the story you carry about who you are. Between a falling glass and a falling opinion of yourself.

To the bio-loop, a threat is a threat.

The word is already out of your mouth. The text is already sent. The door is already slammed. The action follows before the deliberation arrives — and then the deliberation arrives to find the landscape already altered.

This is not a malfunction. It is ancient machinery spinning in conditions it was never designed for. The body that was optimized to outrun a predator is now navigating a performance review, a relationship rupture, a social media silence, a slow accumulation of unmet needs that have no predator to run from and no action that will make them stop.

So the signal follows its established pathways.

It presses harder. It reaches further. It finds the next available channel. Just not always toward what would meet the source.

And the residue accumulates.

Not all of the bio-loop's signals move at the speed of a flinch. Some move slowly — building across hours, accumulating over days, shaping the weather of the week before they are ever noticed directly.

The heaviness from the argument this morning is still shaping this afternoon. The signal for belonging doesn't always arrive in a spike. It is a slow faucet dripping in another room. Only noticeable when the noise drops long enough for it to be heard. The need for meaning may not announce itself as an existential crisis. It may arrive as flatness. A Sunday afternoon feeling that has spread across the whole week.

The bio-loop's fast signals get fed continuously. The slow ones need time.

They need the unoccupied pause in which the slow signal can finally arrive. The pause that has been steadily eliminated by efficiency, and steadily filled by what efficiency has produced. The phone. The screen. The next thing. The next task. The next small relief.

The slow signal continues to transmit. What is missing is somewhere quiet enough for it to land.

And when a signal goes unattended long enough, it can stop feeling like a signal. It starts feeling like the self.

The executive who built a life that looks exactly like success and feels inexplicably hollow inside no longer says *I feel empty*. He says *I am empty. This is who I am*. The bio-loop was spinning toward something real. But the need never fully surfaced. The action continued in the direction culture provided — status, notoriety, the performance of arrival. The hollowness accumulated until it stopped feeling like a signal pointing toward something missing. It became his personality. His personal reality. His verdict on himself.

The person in the relationship that has been quietly wrong for years no longer says *something feels off between us*. She says *I am someone who can't connect. I am too much*. Or *I am not enough*. The low-grade signals — the dissatisfaction, the conversations that almost go somewhere and then don't — spun long enough without being attended to until she stopped reading them as information. They became her identity. The story she tells herself about what kind of person she is.

The person for whom the storm is not an event but a climate stopped asking *why do I feel this way* a long time ago.

They don't feel this way anymore. They are this way.

The signal that was always pointing at something real — a need that has never been properly addressed — became the architecture of an entire life. Not something they carry.

Something they are.

The bio-loop spins faithfully. Legibility is what is missing. Legibility restores the distance between the signal and the self, the crucial distance between *I feel* and *I am*.

That is exactly what the Compass exists to find. A coordinate.

A way to notice that what has felt like identity may have begun as information. A way to hear the signal before it has to become weather. A way to ask whether the action forming now is serving the source or only quieting the noise.

The bio-loop sends a signal through the pathways available — pressing harder, reaching further, finding the easiest route. It is not broken. It is faithful. The signal has been pointing at something real.

Eventually the residue accumulates into harsher weather. It stops being an event and becomes a climate. That is what an unattended bio-loop produces.

Faithfulness without a Compass.

— Explored

The question of what human beings need — and in what order — has a familiar answer.

Maslow's hierarchy, as it is commonly taught, suggests a sequence: first survival, then safety, then belonging, then esteem, then self-actualization. The implication is developmental — meet the lower needs, and the higher ones come online. The person ascends.

Looking at the bio-loop tells a different story.

The needs do not wait their turn.

They spin simultaneously, all of them, generating signals from the beginning. Survival does not finish before belonging begins. Safety does not complete before meaning starts to matter. The infant does not need food first and contact later. The person does not become a meaning-making creature only after every bodily need is secured.

The hierarchy is a useful image for some purposes. Inside the storm, another image may serve better.

The hierarchy is not a ladder.

It is a mixing board.

Every Signal Spinning

All the channels on the mixing board are live.

But what the bio-loop is composing is not a sequence of isolated tracks. It is a symphony — layered, simultaneous, each channel contributing something the others cannot. What varies between channels is not only volume. It is tempo, duration, and what each voice requires to resolve.

Some channels move in staccato.

The neural spike. The flinch. The hand already moving. The word already out of the mouth before the thought has finished forming. Fast, brief, percussive. The signal fires, the action happens, the channel quiets. These are the channels the modern environment feeds most readily: spike after spike, alert after alert, urgency after urgency, keeping the fast passages perpetually active.

Some channels move in long, sustained tones.

The stress chemistry building across minutes, clearing across hours. The gut's chemistry shaping the baseline across days. The heaviness from the argument this morning still sounding in the afternoon. The heart's rhythm encoding the organism's emotional state in patterns that swell and recede gradually, the way a cello line moves beneath everything else without announcing itself.

The loneliness that has been present for weeks before it becomes audible as loneliness. The exhaustion that has been mistaken for irritability. The meaning-signal that arrives as flatness before it ever becomes a question.

These voices don't spike. They build. They linger. They are still sounding when the fast passages have long since resolved. And they require something the staccato channels don't: time. The held pause in which the sustained tone can finally be heard beneath the noise of everything moving faster.

And some voices cannot resolve within the instrument alone.

Hunger is a phrase the organism can often complete — reach, eat, quiet. Belonging is different. Mattering is different. Recognition is different. These signals require reception. A face. A response. A relationship. Another person present enough to answer what the bio-loop is sending.

Some needs depend on response from outside the organism in ways survival needs do not. You can drink water alone. You cannot belong alone. You cannot matter to someone by yourself.

This is why unattended signals can become so confusing. Some are loud and immediate. Some are quiet and persistent. Some can be met by action. Some require response. Some are easy to name. Some arrive disguised.

The mixing board is always live. The question is never whether the signals are generating. The question is whether the signals are being received, whether the responses available actually meet the needs, and what they have learned to reach for when the signals don't subside.

Relief and Resolution

A proxy is an action through any channel that quiets the signal without reaching the source.

It may be harmless in the moment. It may even be useful for a time. A snack when the body needs food. A screen when the mind needs rest. A purchase when the person needs a sense of movement. A plan when uncertainty feels intolerable. An argument when the pressure needs somewhere to go.

The issue is simple: relief can arrive before resolution.

The body senses relief quickly. Repair takes longer to know. Many patterns begin there: a signal finds the nearest available channel, and the body remembers that, for a moment, the pressure went down.

The next time the signal rises, the old channel is easier to find. The bag of chips, the phone, the fantasy, the performance, the withdrawal, the apology, the over-explanation, the accusation, the achievement, the control move. The body has evidence that the pathway does something. The signal quieted once. So the pathway becomes more available.

Over time, a person may begin reaching for the proxy faster than they can feel the need underneath it. The reach becomes familiar. The relief becomes expected. The source remains untouched.

That is how residue accumulates.

The body keeps moving. It keeps reaching. It keeps finding ways to lower pressure. But the unmet need continues to generate signal. The person becomes tired in a specific way — tired from effort that does not reach the source.

A lot of patterns begin there.

Before It Has a Name

Needs, in the full human sense, are not always obvious. Thirst is one of the bio-loop's more legible signals — it points directly at its source and its solution. Many human needs are less clean.

The need for connection does not always announce itself as loneliness. It may arrive as irritability, or as a restless dissatisfaction that attaches itself to whatever is nearby — the relationship, the job, the body, the weather. It may show up as envy, criticism, or a sudden conviction that everyone else is the problem.

The need for meaning does not always arrive as an existential crisis. It arrives as a vague flatness. A Sunday afternoon feeling that has spread across the whole week.

The need for safety does not always look like fear. It may look like control — the elaborately managed environment, the rigid schedule, the disproportionate response to small disruptions, the exhausting vigilance that the person maintaining it experiences as simply the way things need to be.

The need for rest does not always feel like tiredness. It may feel like resentment. Like disgust. Like failure. Like the sudden inability to care about things the person usually values.

The need for grief may not arrive as tears. It may arrive as numbness, distraction, impatience, or a strange anger at ordinary life for continuing.

The bio-loop is signaling. The need is real. But the signal has traveled through story, habit, history, expectation, shame, and whatever channels have been available before. By then, the original need may be hard to hear.

The person responds to what is loudest. Understandably. The loudest thing is the signal as it presents, not necessarily the source that generated it.

So the person manages the irritability, controls the room, eats the food, opens the screen, sends the text, avoids the conversation, performs competence, makes another plan.

Something happens. Something quiets. The question underneath remains.

What was this signal pointing toward before it became this loud?

That is the question unattended signals make difficult. It is also the question the Compass exists to keep available.

The Verdict

The signal-becomes-identity move has a structure underneath it.

When a need has gone unanswered long enough, the organism may stop expecting the signal to point anywhere useful. The signal still transmits, but the person has learned to treat it as a condition of self rather than information from the self.

I am anxious no longer means anxiety is present. It means anxiety has become the room. I am empty no longer means something in the organism is signaling absence. It means emptiness has become the verdict. I am broken no longer means a signal is asking to be understood. It means the conclusion has arrived before the question can form.

Martin Seligman's research into learned helplessness gives one useful window into this pattern. When repeated efforts do not change the conditions that cause distress, organisms can stop attempting responses that might later become available. The learning generalizes. What began as an accurate reading of one situation can become the posture carried into the next.

The bio-loop is still signaling. But the organism has stopped believing the signal points toward anything that can be addressed.

This is the architecture beneath the verdicts.

I am anxious is not a description of the current moment. It is a foreclosure on the possibility that the anxiety points at anything actionable.

I am broken is not a self-assessment based on evidence. It is the organism's adaptive surrender after enough attempts at addressing the signal have produced no resolution.

The signal continues to transmit. The reaching has stopped. The organism has concluded that the reaching does not work, and the conclusion has hardened into identity.

The bio-loop is still spinning underneath. The need is still present. The signal is still transmitting. But the signal is no longer legible as information.

Once the signal has become identity, it becomes harder to answer. A need can be attended to. A signal can be listened to. A pattern can be investigated. A verdict about the self becomes the room the person is living inside.

The anxious person avoids the places where anxiety might speak. The empty person performs arrival and wonders why arrival never lands. The unwanted person scans every room for evidence. The unsafe person organizes life around control and calls it wisdom.

The storm becomes climate.

It has become the weather inside. Persistent. Apparently unnavigable. You dress for it. You do not try to change it. You have forgotten that it is a signal. You have forgotten that signals point at things.

Some of what presents as depressive weather may include this architecture — the signal continues, but the possibility that it points anywhere actionable has collapsed. The bio-loop is now spinning in a closed room. The signal is bouncing off the walls.

The actual need has become invisible and inaccessible beneath the noise of the signal it keeps generating. The discouragement that comes from a need never being properly addressed is debilitating. Understandably so.

That is one of the most painful things unattended signals can do. They can become the atmosphere in which a person learns to live. It is the day spent weeding a garden and then waking up the next day in a garden full of weeds. Day after day. After day.

The Compass preserves a distinction the storm can erase: I feel is not the same sentence as I am.

That distinction may be small at first. It may feel thin. But it matters. It creates the first possible distance between the signal and the self. A signal can be listened to. A verdict can only be lived under.

Why the Compass Goes Quiet

There is a biological reason the Compass goes quiet exactly when the storm gets loud.

The capacities needed to read it are state-dependent. Attention, reflection, memory, symbolic language, and future-oriented choice are easier to access when we have enough room to hold them. Under heavier load, that room shrinks. Attention narrows. Time compresses. Options feel fewer. Nuance becomes harder to carry.

The body prepares for immediacy. Move. Defend. Appease. Explain. Grab. Leave. Shut down. Push through. The Compass has not failed. The conditions for reading it have changed.

Some nervous-system models describe this as a shift in state. Polyvagal theory, for example, gives language to movement between social engagement, mobilization, and shutdown. The Compass does not depend on that theory, and the bio-loop is not explained by it. But the language can be useful because it describes something many people recognize from the inside: under enough pressure, the capacities that make reflection possible become harder to reach.

This is why shame after the fact can be so misleading. A person looks back from a more available state and judges the less available state as if the same capacities were present in both.

I knew better. Why didn't I do better?

Knowing better afterward is different from having access to the bearings under pressure. In the storm, **I Think** — the ability to notice the story as story — may collapse into certainty or disappear into action. **I Need** — the capacity to discern what is actually required — may be mistaken for urge. **I Will** — the availability of intentional action — may compress into **I Do**, action already underway. **I Feel** may flood the whole field or flatten into nothing.

The bio-loop is still spinning. The signals are still generating. The need is still pressing. But the instrument has become difficult to hold.

Reading it becomes easier when the nervous system has recovered enough availability to hold it. What changes is legibility.

That is what is at stake in an unattended bio-loop. The longer signals go unseen, the more pressure accumulates. The more pressure accumulates, the harder the Compass becomes to hold. The harder the Compass becomes to hold, the more likely action is to follow the nearest available channel.

The storm feeds the conditions that make it harder to read.

What Still Holds

Some legibility can return. Usually not all at once. Usually not by force. Often not in the moment when the storm is loudest. But the system can encounter different conditions.

A breath that no longer has to be managed. A face that doesn't flinch. A room with less demand in it. A little more time. A signal named accurately enough that it is no longer entirely alone. A need recognized with less judgment. An action that serves the source more closely than the old channel did. Each one of these can matter.

The Compass does not command the bio-loop. It does not stabilize the organism by force of insight. It does not guarantee that naming the signal will make the need answerable. Its contribution is legibility. When legibility is available, the signal has a little more chance of being heard as signal. The need has a little more chance of being named nearer to its source. The action forming has a little more chance of being seen before it becomes the only available channel.

The bio-loop that has been spinning unattended for years does not return to legibility overnight. But some legibility can return. More often than despair predicts.

The organism that learned to read the environment as dangerous can, through repeated encounters with safety, begin to receive different evidence. The Compass does not command that revision. It clarifies the encounter. The signal can be heard instead of abandoned. The need can be recognized instead of judged. The action may have more room than the nearest available channel. Different conditions are present now, and the bio-loop has different conditions to answer.

What has been lived under can sometimes be heard again as information. The Compass begins there. With legibility.

A small distance between the storm and the one standing in it.

For the full theoretical account of how need hierarchies map onto the bio-loop, the clinical literature on proxies and signal displacement, and the neurological basis for why reflective capacity narrows under load — that material is available at https://waynegwilliams.com/

CHAPTER 4 — What We've Tried

Keep doing what's working. Here's something that may help when it doesn't.

Over several years working in child welfare, including time on inpatient units with children in acute crisis and enduring chronic difficulties, I witnessed real suffering. I wanted to help. That was not in question. Neither was the intention of the clinicians and therapists around me — they wanted to help too. But I kept watching children who were genuinely beginning to find some footing, who were calming, settling, becoming present in their own bodies, go into a therapy session and return significantly more dysregulated than before. Sometimes for hours. Sometimes longer. Then the cycle would begin again.

I sometimes felt like I was rearranging the lounge chairs on the Titanic. Helpless. Watching a vessel go down while the professionals around me appeared to be busying themselves counting lifeboats.

That was my perception at the time. It is obvious to me now, that there were real improvements being made. I can recall many successes. But I still viscerally felt the gaps.

Especially when the children kept cycling.

I still feel the particular grief of someone who wanted to help and could not find the instrument that would actually reach where the signal lived.

That feeling did not leave me. It became the question I could not stop asking.

There are plenty of things that do help, tremendously, when they are available.

Whatever has helped — the therapy, the medication, the practice, the meeting, the book, the conversation — keep doing them. The Compass sits alongside all of it. One more instrument. Additive.

It is most useful in the gaps.

The therapy session is one hour. The rest of the week is something else entirely. The meeting on Wednesday evening soothes and strengthens resolve. The medication manages the volume. The practice helps when it is accessible. Every approach that has ever helped found something real. But each one operates inside a container — an appointment, a session, a practice window, a room with other people in it.

The gaps are where most of life is actually lived. The 4 a.m. wakefulness. The car after the appointment. An ordinary afternoon when nothing is on fire and nothing is navigable. The moment before the door gets slammed — when there is still, barely, a breath between the signal and the action. The moment after, when the reflection arrives to find the landscape already altered.

The Compass lives in those gaps. Alongside whatever is already working. Available when the containers are not.

In my decades-long search for something that would help me see more clearly, I explored widely and tried more than a few: psychology, philosophy, religion, therapy, meditation, manifestation, psychedelics, nootropics, and other mind-altering approaches that seemed promising. Some helped. A few helped profoundly. None felt complete. They mostly felt like someone else's interpretation of what they thought might be the answer to a question I was not asking.

What I wanted was both simpler and harder than any of them offered.

I wanted to understand myself — not as a diagnosis, not as a collection of symptoms or patterns or traumas, not as something broken that needed to be fixed, but as a human being traversing a mortal life. Making choices under constraints I did not fully comprehend. Guided by something that was both part of me and somehow distinct from me.

Each approach that has ever helped found a real piece of the bio-loop. The bio-loop is the whole organism, all the time, in every condition — including the conditions outside every container. If you have tried things and still feel something missing, the approaches were doing what they could. You may simply be standing where the instruments weren't designed to reach.

The Compass is what we carry into that gap.

An instrument small enough to hold when the signal is loud and the ground is hard to find. It does one thing well.

It locates.

When we are located, we're not lost.

— Explored

The last hundred and fifty years have produced an extraordinary range of attempts to address human suffering. Most of them found something real. Each one also reached an edge — the point where the storm crossed into territory the approach wasn't built to map.

That edge is not a verdict on the approach. It is the nature of the territory. The bio-loop is the whole organism, all the time, in every condition. Every approach found a piece of it. No single piece was the whole.

The person who has tried several of them and still feels something missing is standing at a structural edge. The approach reached its limit. That is different from failing the approach.

Understanding where the edges are makes the gap legible.

Psychiatric diagnosis and medication found that biology matters — that the brain is an organ and chemistry shapes experience. That contribution is real, and medication has kept people alive who would not otherwise have survived the signal's volume. What diagnosis does not reliably do is locate what the signal is pointing toward. Naming the pattern is not the same as attending to what generated it. A person can become less symptomatic and still remain profoundly lost.

The story-focused approaches — particularly cognitive behavioral work — found that the narrative the mind tells about experience shapes the response to it, and that the narrative can be examined and sometimes revised. That is real and has helped many people. The edge appears when the thought is not distorted. When the loneliness is genuine. When the absence of felt meaning is not just a distorted thought. You cannot restructure your way out of a need the bio-loop is faithfully signaling. The thought is not always the problem.

The contemplative traditions, migrated into clinical practice as mindfulness, found the ground — the capacity to observe experience rather than being fused with it. That is the precondition for using the Compass and it is not a small thing. The edge appears when observation stops there. Presence changes the relationship to the signal. It does not by itself tell the person what the signal is pointing toward.

The body-centered approaches came closest to the bio-loop's own language. They understood that the signal runs faster than the narrative, that the body carries what the story has already explained and moved past, and that a therapy working only through cognition is working one floor above where part of the problem lives. Their edge is practical rather than theoretical: the depth of work they do requires a container, a trained guide, and careful pacing. The body's most difficult material does not always yield safely without support.

The motivational approaches found something important about agency — that intention cannot be installed from outside, that the person has to hear their own reasons. The edge appears when the behavior being changed is still answering a need that has not found another path. A sincere intention on Tuesday can still have gravitational force pulling against it by Thursday, because the need the behavior was serving did not disappear when the intention formed.

The recovery rooms found something many clinical approaches never reproduced at scale: the bio-loop carries its signal differently when the signal is no longer borne alone. People sat in a circle, told the truth, and were received by others who knew the signal from the inside — not as diagnosis, not as case, but as recognition. When the signal was genuinely received, something happened in the person that no individual act of self-knowledge could produce. The rooms found that the bio-loop was never designed to carry everything by itself. Their edge is calibration — the instrument is built for a particular family of storms, and it behaves differently in different weather.

The self-help shelf deserves more respect than it often receives.

It is easy to mock the genre — the promises, the formulas, the bright covers, the language of transformation repeated until the word itself becomes thin. Some of that criticism is earned. A great deal has been packaged too quickly, promised too loudly, and sold to people in pain as if the right book, the right habit, the right morning routine, the right mindset, or the right system could finally make them into the person they were supposed to become.

But that is not the whole story. Not even close.

At its best, self-help recognized something the professional world has often been slow to honor: most people do not live their lives inside treatment rooms. They suffer in kitchens, bedrooms, cars, workplaces, marriages, churches, grocery store aisles, and at three in the morning when no clinician is available. They need language they can carry. They need frameworks that do not require permission to use. They need some way to understand their own experience without first becoming a patient, a case, or a diagnosis.

That impulse is not shallow. It is humane.

The best self-help books have given people exactly that. A sentence that named something they had carried for years. A framework that made their behavior feel less like defect and more like pattern. A practice that created a little more room. A story that made loneliness survivable because someone else had apparently stood in the same weather and found words for it.

Sometimes a book reaches a person before therapy can. Sometimes it gives them enough dignity to stop interpreting their suffering as private failure.

That deserves honor.

The limitation is not the impulse. The limitation is the tendency of portable maps to become universal maps.

A book finds something real. Attachment. Habit. Trauma. Mindset. Shame. Discipline. Nervous-system activation. Meaning. Grief. Purpose. Boundaries. Desire. The inner child. The body. The story. The soul. Any one of these can be a real window into the storm. Sometimes the window is so clean, so urgently needed, that when the reader first sees through it, everything changes.

For a while.

That is the self-help experience millions of people know intimately: the book that changed everything for six weeks. The underlining. The new language. The relief of finally having a frame. The sense that this is it — the missing piece. And then, slowly or suddenly, the old pattern returns. Not always in the same clothes. Sometimes it has learned the new language. Sometimes it now quotes the book. But the storm is still there, and the reader concludes what the genre too often trains them to conclude:

I failed again.

I did not practice it correctly. I did not want it badly enough. I know better and still cannot do better.

That is where self-help can become cruel without meaning to. Not because the insight was false, but because the promise around it was too large. A partial instrument was handed to a whole person in a whole storm, and when it could not read every dimension of that storm, the failure landed back on the reader.

This book is not exempt from that danger.

It also offers a portable instrument. It also uses simple language. It also risks being mistaken for a method, a formula, or the final missing piece. So the boundary has to be said clearly: the Compass is not a life system. It is not a cure. It is not a substitute for therapy, medicine, community, spiritual life, material change, or help from other people. It does not promise transformation. It does not make the storm stop.

It locates.

That is the difference this book is trying to preserve. Not superiority over the self-help canon, but restraint inside the same terrain. The Compass is meant to be small enough to carry precisely because no book can carry the whole life of the person reading it.

The standard approaches share a common theme across all their differences.

Each one works inside a container — a session, an appointment, a meeting, a practice window. Each container is real and can be life-giving. But the conditions that make the container necessary are not confined to the hours when the container is present.

The storm is there on an ordinary afternoon. In the car after the appointment. In the kitchen, in the argument, in the waiting room. At three in the morning when the signal is loudest and no one else is available.

The person who has done the somatic work and sat in the rooms and taken the medication and read the books and made genuine progress — who is measurably better — can still find themselves, on an ordinary afternoon, unable to tell where they are.

That person is not a treatment failure.

They may simply be standing in a storm the available instruments were not built to navigate alone.

The Compass is what you carry into that storm. A way to locate where you are while anything else that helps becomes possible again.

For the full account of what each approach found, where its structural edges lie, and how the bio-loop maps onto the clinical literature — that material is available at https://waynegwilliams.com/

PART TWO: THE GROUND

CHAPTER 5 — The Mind

Mind, named by function rather than essence: the mediating layer where body signal, story closure, and the deeper orientation toward what is actually present become distinguishable enough for navigation. Holds the Compass.

The word *mind* carries too much history to be handled casually.

Philosophers have argued over it for centuries. Religious traditions have placed it in different relationships to soul, spirit, body, and self. Psychologists have studied its patterns. Neuroscientists have traced its dependence on the brain. Regular people use the word every day without needing to settle any of that: *my mind is racing; I changed my mind; I can't get it out of my mind; part of me knows better.*

We do not need to solve the whole mystery.

We only need to ask a narrower question:

What is the mind doing when the storm is happening?

When the bio-loop is signaling, when the body is tightening, when a story is forming, when action is gathering itself before we have fully chosen it — what is the layer in which all of that becomes noticeable?

We are not defining mind by what it ultimately is.

We are defining mind by what it does inside the storm.

Mind names the mediating layer where the body's signal, the story's need for closure, and the deeper orientation toward what is true can become available to one another. The purpose is not control. It is legibility. The body keeps its signal. The story can be seen as story. Attention has somewhere truthful to rest. Action gains more room than urgency allowed.

So the signal can be distinguished from the story. So the need can be approached beneath the urgency. So action can be rejoined to authorship before the nearest available channel becomes the only one.

The mind does not regulate the bio-loop.

It holds the Compass.

There are moments when I can hear myself becoming a story before I can stop it.

A feeling rises. The body tightens. A phrase attaches itself to the feeling and begins explaining it. The explanation is fast, persuasive, almost complete by the time I notice it. Someone did something. Something is wrong. A situation must be handled. The story arrives with the force of reality because the body has already given it urgency.

And somewhere inside that same event, something else is present.

The body is signaling. The story is closing. Action is already gathering itself. And some part of me can notice the whole assembly beginning to move.

That noticing is easy to misattribute as control.

It is not control.

If noticing were control, we would simply stop. We would see the pattern and decline to repeat it. We would watch the storm gather and choose clear weather.

That is not how it works.

The mind is not the captain standing above the body with a wheel in its hands. It is the place where the body's reports, the story's explanations, and the possibility of deliberate action become available to one another. Sometimes clearly. Sometimes poorly. Sometimes too late to stop the first movement, but not too late to understand what happened.

The only instrument available for examining the mind is the mind itself.

That is the difficulty. It is easier to demonstrate than explain.

Try it now, if you are willing. Turn attention toward what your mind is doing. Watch for the next thought.

What happens?

The attempt to watch becomes part of what is being watched. The effort enters the frame. The original thought — the one that was there before you turned to look — recedes. Not gone. Simply harder to see directly. Like looking in a mirror to catch something directly behind your head. You know it is still there. You just cannot see it because now you are in the way.

Now stop trying so hard.

Let the thoughts come without reaching for them.

A concern from earlier. A fragment of a song. A sudden inventory of everything that needs doing. A sentence forming before you chose it. Each one arrives with the quiet insistence of something that expects to be followed.

And then, sometimes, a little space appears.

The thought is here.

It belongs to me.

It is moving through my mind.

It is not the whole of me.

And it is not necessarily true.

There are two movements happening here, and distinguishing them matters for everything that follows.

The first is automatic operation. Thoughts arriving without invitation. The story machine running its continuous narrative — predicting, remembering, rehearsing, evaluating, warning, explaining. Left to its own momentum, this is what the mind does. It generates story. It processes the past. It anticipates the future. The ongoing commentary most people experience as thinking is this machinery running.

The second is deliberate orientation. The capacity to notice that a thought has arrived. To notice that a story is running. To notice that a feeling is present before the story has finished explaining it. To let attention settle enough that signal and story are no longer fused into one undifferentiated weather system.

Deliberate orientation is not control. It does not stop automatic operation. It does not prevent thoughts from arriving, feelings from rising, or stories from forming. It changes what becomes visible while they are happening.

That visibility is what the Compass needs.

The mind holds the Compass.

The bio-loop is what the Compass reads — the body's signal about what it requires. I Am is the ground from which the storm can be held without becoming the whole self. Mind is the mediating layer between them: the place where the instrument can be held, where the signal can be attended to, where the story can be seen as story, and where action can begin to belong to the one taking it.

Attention is the mind's aperture.

Whatever we turn attention toward becomes foreground. Everything else recedes. Left to automatic operation, attention usually narrows toward whatever is loudest — and what is loudest is often the story the mind is already telling about the signal, not the signal itself.

Curiosity is the orientation that keeps attention honest.

Not curiosity as novelty, analysis, or the hunger to explain. Curiosity here means the willingness to remain turned toward what is actually happening before the closure-story finishes deciding what is there. The bio-loop closes fast. Curiosity is not faster. It is simply still available after the closing has begun — able to notice that a story has formed before the signal was fully heard.

A bio-loop approached with curiosity has room to speak.

A bio-loop approached with a conclusion already formed can only answer inside the conclusion. The verdict has arrived before the signal has had room to show what it was carrying.

The question *what is this?* is a curiosity question.

It keeps the aperture open.

The question *why does this keep happening?* often does something else. It begins answering itself before the bio-loop has had a chance to speak.

The difference between the two questions is the difference between navigation and verdict.

When attention turns toward the bio-loop's signal — toward I Feel — the mind shifts from automatic operation toward deliberate orientation. From generating story to observing signal. From being carried by the narrative to noticing that a narrative is present.

This shift is the whole maneuver.

The chapters that follow will use this directly. I Feel asks attention to turn toward the signal. I Need asks attention to stay close enough to locate what the signal is pointing toward. I Think asks attention to notice the story and see it as story rather than territory. I Will / I Do asks attention to notice the space between intention and action, and whether action still belongs to the one taking it.

Each bearing requires deliberate orientation — the capacity to turn toward what is present without fusing completely with the story already running about it.

This route can become more familiar.

The two movements you just distinguished — the one that arrives without invitation and the one that can notice it is arriving — are the architecture the Compass works inside. The automatic still runs. It will keep running. But deliberate orientation becomes easier to find. The switching becomes more available.

The mind learns the feel of the instrument.

— In Brief

Mind is named here by function. It is the mediating layer where body signal, story, attention, and action become distinguishable enough for navigation.

Most of the time, mind runs on automatic. Thoughts arrive. Stories generate. The narrative continues. This is the default pattern.

The Compass becomes readable through deliberate orientation: the capacity to notice what is happening without becoming fused with it.

Attention is the mind's aperture: whatever it turns toward becomes foreground.

Curiosity keeps the aperture open. The willingness to stay turned toward what is present before the story closes.

Curiosity is capacity-dependent. Under enough load, we reach for closure. When curiosity is available, the Compass becomes easier to read.

Mind holds the Compass. Attention turns it. Curiosity keeps it open. Legibility makes navigation possible.

— Explored

What We Mean by Mind

What is the mind?

The question has occupied philosophy for millennia, religious traditions for longer still, and neuroscience with increasing precision in recent decades. No single answer has settled the matter. That should make us careful.

The Compass does not require a final theory of mind. It does not require us to decide whether mind is reducible to brain, emergent from body, continuous with soul, grounded in awareness, or best understood through some other account entirely.

It requires something narrower.

We need to know what the mind is doing when the storm is happening.

When the bio-loop is signaling, when the body is tightening, when a story begins closing around the signal, when action is already gathering before we have fully chosen it — what is the layer in which those movements become available to one another?

That is the sense in which we will use the word *mind*.

Mind is the mediating layer where body signal, story closure, attention, and action become distinguishable enough for navigation.

The brain is a biological organ. It processes information, coordinates responses, stores and retrieves patterns, predicts, reacts, and participates in everything we are describing. Nothing here asks us to dismiss the brain.

But the Compass is not asking you to examine the brain as an organ. It is asking you to notice the lived field in which signals, stories, attention, and action become available. We are calling that field mind.

The mind is also distinct from I Am. I Am names the ground from which the storm can be held without becoming the whole self. Mind is more active, more changeable, more involved in the weather. It is where the story runs, where attention turns, where the signal can be noticed or missed, where urgency can close too quickly, and where action can begin to belong again to the one taking it.

When we say "the mind holds the Compass," we mean this:

The Compass becomes readable through the layer where body signal can be noticed, story can be seen as story, need can become more legible, and action can be rejoined to authorship.

This is less abstract than it sounds.

There are moments when you can hear yourself becoming a story before you can stop it. A feeling rises. The body tightens. A phrase attaches itself to the feeling and begins explaining it. The explanation is fast, persuasive, almost complete by the time you notice it.

And somewhere inside that same event, something else is present.

The body is signaling. The story is closing. Action is gathering. And something in you can notice the assembly beginning to move.

That noticing is easy to mistake for control.

If noticing were control, the storm would gather and we would choose otherwise.

That is not quite how it works.

Noticing changes the encounter. It does not control, but it does change it. The story is still running, but it can be seen as story. The signal is still present, but it may no longer be completely swallowed by the explanation attached to it. The action may already be gathering, but a small space can open around it.

That small space is where the Compass becomes possible.

Prediction and Story

The mind is not neutral glass.

By the time a feeling becomes noticeable, the brain has often already begun predicting what the signal means. The body is reporting. The brain is modeling. The story is beginning to form. Mind is where all of this becomes experience.

Predictive-processing research gives useful language for this. The brain is not only receiving information from the world and body. It is also generating expectations about what that information means. Incoming signals meet existing predictions, and experience forms inside that meeting. In ordinary life, this is what lets the world become usable quickly enough for action. We do not build reality from scratch each moment. We meet it through models already in motion.

For the Compass, this matters because the mind we are using to read the bio-loop is already interpreting. When attention turns inward toward a feeling, a need, or a body report, it is not encountering untouched data. It is encountering experience already shaped by what we have learned to expect.

The story machine is one expression of this architecture.

It takes what the bio-loop is signaling and begins predicting what the signal means, what caused it, what will happen next, what must be done, and who is responsible. By the time the signal reaches conscious awareness, the prediction is often already running. The feeling arrives wearing an explanation.

That does not make the story false. It means the story is doing work before we have noticed it working.

This is why I Think has to become visible as I Think. The story is not the enemy. It gathers memory into continuity, lets the future be rehearsed, and helps identity hold across time. It is one of the ways the mind keeps a life coherent. The difficulty begins when the story is mistaken for the signal itself.

The Compass does not give us raw access beneath prediction. It gives us a way to notice that prediction is already here.

That noticing matters.

It is the beginning of navigation.

The Story Machine at Rest

The brain at rest is not idle.

The discovery of what came to be called the Default Mode Network helped make this visible. When attention is not captured by an external task, the mind goes to work on its own. It replays conversations. It imagines what might happen. It rehearses what should have been said. It models other people. It maintains the thread of self across time.

The story machine is doing its job.

This is one reason quiet moments can become noisy. When the external demand drops, the narrative often returns. The hands stop moving. The task ends. The phone goes down. The pause opens. Then the mind resumes its internal work.

For some people, that return is creative or reflective. For others, it is painful. The narrative comes back with accusation, regret, prediction, comparison, rehearsal, or dread. The body sends a signal, and the story machine begins fitting it into an old pattern.

This is not a defect in the mind. It is part of what minds do. They remember, anticipate, compare, explain, and prepare. Those capacities help human beings survive and belong. They also make it possible for an old story to arrive so quickly that it feels like reality.

For the Compass, the important point is simple: the pause does not automatically create clarity. Sometimes the pause lets the story machine get louder.

That is why attention matters.

The signal may be present. The story may be running.

The Compass becomes useful when mind can notice both.

Automatic Operation and Deliberate Orientation

The Compass asks the mind to shift orientation.

The default pattern is automatic operation. Thoughts arrive without invitation. Stories generate. The narrative continues. The mind predicts, remembers, rehearses, evaluates, warns, explains. Much of this happens before deliberate choice has entered the room.

Automatic operation is necessary. A person could not function if every thought, prediction, association, and bodily response required conscious permission. The mind is always doing more than awareness can supervise.

But reading the bio-loop requires the other movement.

Deliberate orientation is the capacity to notice what has arrived. A thought is here. A story is forming. A feeling is present. An urge is gathering. A need may be underneath this. An action is beginning to take shape.

This orientation does not stop automatic operation. It makes automatic operation more visible.

That difference matters.

Spontaneous mind wandering and deliberate inward attention are not the same experience. In one, the mind is carried by whatever association, memory, worry, image, or prediction becomes active next. In the other, attention turns toward something because it needs to be noticed. Both are internal. Both may involve story. Their lived feel is different.

The Compass depends on the second movement.

The bio-loop is always signaling, but reading it is not usually the default.

The default is often the story about the signal.

I am anxious.
Something is wrong.
This always happens.
I need to do something.

Deliberate orientation turns toward the report itself.

Something is constricting in my chest.
There is heat in my face.
My body is bracing.
My stomach has dropped.

The signal becomes available as signal, rather than only as the story already forming around it.

This is not a clean switch from one system to another. The mind is more interwoven than that. Automatic story and deliberate orientation overlap, interrupt each other, and cooperate in complicated ways. Still, the distinction matters for lived navigation. A mind that can move, even briefly, from being carried by the story to noticing that a story is present has more available than a mind fully fused with whatever has become most salient.

Each time attention turns toward the bio-loop's signal rather than remaining wholly inside the story about the signal, the route becomes more familiar.

The automatic still runs. The story still forms.

Deliberate orientation becomes easier to find.

And when it does, the Compass has room to work.

Attention and Curiosity

Attention is the mind's aperture.

Whatever attention turns toward becomes foreground. Everything else recedes. This is why attention matters so much inside the storm. Left to automatic operation, attention often narrows toward whatever is loudest. What is loudest may be the body's signal. It may be the story about the signal. It may be the nearest available action. It may be the threat, the accusation, the shame, the plan, the memory, the text, the door.

Attention does not regulate the bio-loop. It changes what becomes available in the field.

Curiosity keeps the aperture from closing too quickly and shapes what comes into sharper focus.

Curiosity provides the willingness to remain turned toward what is actually happening while understanding is still incomplete.

The bio-loop closes fast. It has to. We need enough certainty to act. Under pressure, the story may close around the signal before the signal has been fully heard.

Something is wrong.
This always happens.
I know what this is.
I know what they meant.
I know what I need to do.

Curiosity keeps the aperture open and shapes what within that open field comes into focus.

When the aperture stays open but attention remains unfocused, what sharpens is usually whatever is loudest: the story already forming, the urgency already gathering, the familiar conclusion already arriving. The brain conserves energy by defaulting to what has worked before. The signal is in the field. The story is also in the field. Without curiosity the story usually sharpens first.

Curiosity shifts the focal point. It turns sharper attention toward the signal itself rather than the explanation assembling around it. The body's report has a chance to come into focus before the narrative closes over it.

Curiosity can begin inside fear, anger, suspicion, shame, or bracing. It may be faint. It may last only a moment. But even a small amount can change the encounter.

A frightened attention focuses on threat. It asks: *how do I get away from this?*

An angry attention focuses on cause. It asks: *who is to blame?*

An ashamed attention focuses on self-assessment. It asks: *what does this prove about me?*

A curious attention focuses on the signal itself. It asks: *what is this, actually?*

That question matters because it stays closer to the signal. It does not force the signal to confirm the story already forming around it. It gives the bio-loop more room to report accurately.

The path is reorientation. Fear may still be present. Anger may still be present. The bracing may still be in the body. Curiosity gives attention another way to stand in relation to them. The field is no longer organized only around defense, verdict, or control. Something in the system remains available to what is actually the case.

Familiar orientations have grooves worn deep by years of use. Management returns. Judgment returns. The old explanation reforms. Curiosity develops slowly under pressure, with interruption and return.

But this is what it makes possible:

A bio-loop approached with curiosity has room to be heard.

The signal that has been spinning — sometimes for years, sometimes for decades, sometimes since before there was language for it — may finally have somewhere to land. It can be heard more honestly when the answer has not already taken the signal captive. Attention turns toward it without immediately turning it into accusation, diagnosis, failure, or demand.

The question *what is this?* asked genuinely, with the answer still open, keeps the aperture available. The bio-loop can report. The need can become more legible. The story can become more visible as story.

Why does this keep happening? may sound like inquiry, but often it has already begun to close. The question is answering itself before it completes. The conclusion is forming before the bio-loop has had a chance to report. It can become judgment wearing the costume of a question.

The difference between the two questions is the difference between navigation and verdict.

Curiosity is how attention remains available to what is actually present.

But curiosity needs room to work. Even a breath of unoccupied time — a pause before the reach, a moment before the response completes — is what allows the focal point to shift. Without it, the story closes before curiosity can redirect attention toward the signal. The pause is not passive. It is the condition the other two require.

That is how the Compass gets read.

Reading Is Not Controlling

The mind can read the bio-loop. It cannot control it.

This distinction runs through the entire Compass. The bio-loop is older, faster, and more fundamental than the mind's deliberate operation. It was spinning before language, before reflection, before any conscious story could explain what the organism was doing. It operates on timescales the conscious mind usually encounters only after the fact.

By the time a feeling reaches awareness, the bio-loop is already in motion. By the time the story machine begins explaining the feeling, the signal has already done some of its work.

The mind's access to the bio-loop is partial and delayed. It does not stand at the origin point, watching the signal begin. It usually meets the signal after it has already risen, after the body has already tightened, reached, braced, collapsed, accelerated, or prepared.

And still, partial access is real access. Delayed access is still enough to matter.

The mind can read what the bio-loop is signaling with enough precision to begin distinguishing signal from story. Enough to ask: what is the feeling? What is the body reporting? What need might be underneath it? What is this organism reaching for?

That is already a different encounter.

The signal that had been swallowed by the story becomes more legible. The story that had been mistaken for reality becomes visible as story. The action that had been gathering itself through urgency has more room around it.

The mind does not command the bio-loop into a new state. It changes the encounter by making the bio-loop's report more articulable.

Naming matters here. To articulate what is present — tightness, heat, dread, loneliness, hunger, shame, exhaustion, the need to matter, the reach toward relief — is to introduce more accurate information into the encounter.

We are no longer only having the signal. We are also encountering the signal as something that can be noticed, named, and distinguished from the story around it.

That does not force the signal to change. But it gives the bio-loop more accurate information to respond to.

The Compass is an instrument of observation, not control. Observation changes the encounter. When the mind reads the bio-loop with enough honesty, the signal has somewhere to land. The story has less authority to pretend it is the whole truth. The need has a chance to become more visible than the proxy. Action may have more room than urgency allowed.

The bio-loop keeps spinning. The mind learns to read.

The Faculty That Holds the Instrument

Which brings the inquiry back to the one holding the Compass.

Your body, your brain, even your mind are not the whole of what you are. They are how you encounter the storm.

The body signals. The brain predicts, coordinates, and prepares. The mind mediates, holding body signal, story, attention, and action close enough together that they can become distinguishable.

When we say the mind holds the Compass, we are naming that function.

Attention is the aperture through which the instrument turns. Curiosity is what keeps it open and shapes what comes into focus.

Attention is finite, and it is directable. Whatever attention turns toward becomes foreground. Whatever remains unattended recedes into the weather.

When attention is directed deliberately, the field changes: the signal can be heard more clearly, the story can be seen as story, the need can begin to separate from the proxy, and action has more room than urgency allowed.

When attention drifts toward what is loudest, most familiar, or most urgent, the story machine usually chooses the route. The bio-loop keeps signaling. The mind keeps explaining. Action keeps forming along the nearest available channel.

That is how we move without navigating.

The Compass is in your hand.

Attention is how the instrument turns.

Curiosity helps with focus.

Time, even a breath's worth, is what allows both.

But the Compass is reading signals that begin before opinion, before explanation, before the story machine has finished its work. The body's reports are already in motion by the time the mind begins naming them.

Before the Compass can be used well, those signal sources need to be understood. That is what comes next.

The account of mind offered here is functional — enough to hold the Compass and use it. The deeper neuroscientific warrant, the fuller treatment of attention, narrative, and predictive processing, and the research literature behind the framework will be available at https://waynegwilliams.com/

CHAPTER 6 — Gut, Heart, Head

Gut, heart, and head: three embodied signal centers. Each sends real information into the bio-loop. The gut tends toward body-level need. The heart tends toward affective state. The head narrates, predicts, and explains. Navigation improves when all three are read.

I wasn't sure how, but somehow, I knew that I shouldn't have.

It felt like something was trying to warn me. There didn't seem to be a good reason not to. But I couldn't shake the uneasiness, a certain doubt that I couldn't reason away. There was a pressure beneath the explanation. The hesitation didn't make any sense, so I went ahead and did it.

And once done, I couldn't undo it. Regardless of how badly I wanted to. Over the years, I have learned to trust that feeling.

We have been taught to trust the narrative and manage the sensation. It turns out the inverse may be better advice.

While it may be hard to get an agreement on what exactly the mind is, you are likely to know more about the gut and heart. Their substance, their shape, their edges. You know about their function: the heart pumps blood; the gut processes food. These descriptions are accurate as far as they go.

They don't go very far.

The gut and heart are also sending signals. Constantly. More signals than conscious awareness will ever receive directly. They arrive before the head-brain decides which ones matter, translates them into story, and assigns them meaning.

Through major pathways like the vagus nerve, much of the body's traffic flows upward — the body reporting, the head-brain receiving and responding. The hierarchy we inherited is more reciprocal than we were taught.

These are measurable transmissions, processed through neural, hormonal, immune, vascular, and metabolic pathways, arriving at the head-brain already carrying information about the state of our body and its environment.

The butterflies before the difficult conversation.
The tightening before the news arrives.
The sudden settling when something that felt wrong becomes right.

These are not decorative.

They are the body's reporters filing from the field.

Gut, heart, head.

Three embodied signal centers. Not one commander with two accessories. Three contributors. Three kinds of report. The head is the loudest in language, so we often let it speak for our whole organism. That does not make it the whole organism.

The Five Sentences were not conceptualized out of thin air. They follow the shape of our organism closely enough to be relevant. The gut, heart, and head each contribute different kinds of signal. I Need, I Feel, and I Think are not categories dropped onto the body from above. They name tendencies already present in the way the body reports, evaluates, and interprets its own condition.

The gut tends toward the body-level signal that precedes any named feeling. The pressure that something is required before you know what it is or what to call it. This is Need territory: the bio-loop registering requirement before the thinking mind has arrived to interpret it.

The heart tends toward the body's continuous felt report of its own state. Not rate alone — rhythm. The felt sense of how things are going, encoded in patterns the chest knows before the head has formed a thought about it. This is Feel territory: affective signal, valence, the body's report of what it is experiencing.

The head-brain tends toward story. It takes what the body is already saying and constructs an interpretation around it: narrative, explanation, prediction. Useful when accurate. Costly when mistaken for the signal itself.

None of these tendencies are exclusive. The gut contributes to feeling — **I Feel**. The heart contributes to thought — **I Think**. The head contributes to need — **I Need** — through every story it tells about what must happen next. The organism is always more interwoven than any map can make it.

Still, the tendencies help.

I Am is not one of those signal centers. It is the Compass's True North: the ground from which the whole storm can be held without becoming the whole self.

I Will / I Do is where the reading becomes movement, where the system moves outward.

The Compass reads what the bio-loop has always been signaling.

Sensation often arrives before conscious story. It comes before the interpretation, before the explanation the head-brain will construct around it. That makes sensation earlier data, less translated data, data closer to the body's first report.

The story is downstream. The head-brain receives signals from the gut and heart and translates them so quickly that what reaches awareness is often the translation, not the transmission. The story about the signal rather than the signal itself.

The problem is where attention has been trained to look.

A mind oriented toward the narrative arrives after the story has already begun forming around the signal. The sensation gets explained before it is attended to. The data gets processed into meaning before it has been heard as itself.

Learning to reach the signal before the story machine has finished explaining it away is accurate reading of instruments that have been transmitting longer than language has existed to name them.

Here is the architecture in plain terms.

The gut signals body-level requirement before any named feeling may arrive.

The heart broadcasts the organism's state continuously.

The head-brain interprets what the body is reporting.

The interpretation runs so fast that what reaches awareness is usually the interpretation rather than the signal itself.

Attention can travel beneath the explanation.

Reading all three is what navigation requires.

The head-brain does not need to be silenced.

It needs to be joined by the reports it has been explaining.

The gut sends.

The heart sends.

The head explains.

The Compass teaches the one holding it how to read before the explanation becomes the whole world.

— In Brief

Gut, heart, and head are embodied signal centers. Each sends real information into the bio-loop.

The gut tends toward body-level need: the pressure of requirement before it has a name.

The heart tends toward felt state: the organism's affective report of how things are going.

The head-brain tends toward story: narrative, prediction, explanation, and meaning.

The story arrives quickly. Often it replaces the signal it was built from.

Attention can travel beneath the explanation. When it does, the signal becomes more readable.

The Compass is calibrated for the organism: gut, heart, head, ground, and action;

Need, Feel, Think, I Am, I Will / I Do.

— Explored

You are in a storm.

The weather of being alive has always included body signals, shifting rhythms, pressing needs, and a head-brain trying to explain what all of it means. Most of the time the head-brain narrates that weather so quickly that its explanation feels like the whole event.

It is not the only source of report.

Navigation requires more than narrative management. It requires reading the organism before the story has claimed final authority over it. That means learning where the reports are coming from.

The trail divides here: gut, heart, head. Three embodied signal centers. Each distinct. Each contributing. Each sending information the Compass will need to read if the bearing is going to mean anything.

The gut reports body-level requirement before the need has a name.

The heart reports the organism's felt state before the story has explained it.

The head-brain narrates, predicts, interprets, and prepares action around what the body has already begun sending.

All three are always participating. None speaks alone. The tendencies matter because they help us know where to listen.

We start with the oldest one.

The Gut

The gut is not just digestion.

Hundreds of millions of neurons line the walls of the gastrointestinal tract. Michael Gershon, whose work helped bring this architecture into public view, called it "the second brain." The phrase can be overstated, but the reason it caught on is real: the enteric nervous system operates with considerable independence from the head-brain, coordinating digestion, monitoring the internal environment, and sending information upward through several channels at once.

The vagus nerve is one of the most important of those channels. It is also strikingly lopsided. A large majority of vagal fibers carry signals from body to brain rather than from brain to body. The traffic flows predominantly upward. The gut is reporting. The head-brain is receiving. The hierarchy we inherited — brain commanding, body obeying — becomes much more reciprocal under examination.

The vagus nerve is only one pathway. The gut communicates through neural signaling, the bloodstream, immune activity, hormonal secretions, and microbial metabolites. Some signals move quickly. Others shape baseline slowly across hours or days. Together they form what researchers now call the microbiota-gut-brain axis: a bidirectional communication system linking the gut's internal world with the brain's processing.

That internal world is alive in ways most of us were never taught to imagine. The gut contains trillions of microorganisms living in complex relationship with the human body. They metabolize, ferment, signal, compete, cooperate, and produce compounds the body has to answer. Their activity participates in immune signaling, metabolic state, inflammation, gut integrity, and pathways connected to mood and motivation.

This is where the wonder has to remain careful. The gut is not secretly controlling the mind. Gut serotonin does not simply travel upward and become brain serotonin. The blood-brain barrier keeps the relationship more complex than that. Depression, anxiety, motivation, appetite, ease, and unease cannot be reduced to gut chemistry.

Still, the central point is already strong enough:

The head-brain is not interpreting itself alone.

The neurochemical and inflammatory environment the head-brain receives is shaped by the body beneath it. Gut signaling contributes to the conditions under which mood, energy, vigilance, and motivation become available. The body's baseline state has a chemistry, and part of that chemistry is being shaped below conscious awareness.

Most of what the gut transmits never surfaces as a named sensation. The microbiome's influence, immune signaling, digestive state, metabolic conditions, and continuous monitoring of the internal environment all shape the organism without announcing themselves in words.

But some of the gut's signals do surface.

The butterflies before the difficult conversation. The clench before the decision. The nausea that arrives before the thought catches up. The sudden settling when something that felt wrong becomes right.

These are the legible surface of a deeper architecture.

That is why the gut belongs in this chapter. The Compass does not need to reach the microbiome. It does not need to decode microbial metabolites or trace immune pathways. It only needs to respect that what surfaces as body-level pressure may be connected to a vast field of reporting beneath the reach of conscious thought.

The signals tending toward Need — the body-level urgency, the pressing that has no name yet — are real, readable, and worth attending to.

The head may not know what the gut is saying yet.

That does not mean nothing has been said.

The Heart

The heart began before the head had anything like a story to tell.

In the developing body, the heart starts beating early — before language, before prediction, before anything that could narrate what the organism is becoming. Long before the head-brain can explain, the heart is already pulsing, already establishing one of the body's first rhythms of continuity.

The heart has its own intrinsic nervous system — a network of neurons embedded in and around cardiac tissue, involved in local processing and communication with the central nervous system. It is autorhythmic, meaning the heartbeat begins from within the heart itself. The head-brain can speed it, slow it, modulate it, and respond to it. The heart does not wait for the head to begin.

Place a heart in the right conditions outside the body, and it continues beating.

The heart is not only a pump in the emotional life of the organism. Its rhythm participates in the body-brain conversation through which feeling becomes available. The heart communicates through neural signals traveling upward through vagal and spinal afferents, through hormonal pathways, through pressure feedback as blood moves, and through electrical rhythms measurable at the surface of the body.

The head-brain is receiving the heart continuously.

Beat by beat, pressure receptors fire as blood is ejected. Signals travel upward into regions involved in mapping the body's internal state. This happens beneath awareness, with every beat. The head-brain is not imagining the heart. It is receiving the heart as part of the organism's ongoing report of itself.

Attention can make this report more available.

When attention turns toward the heartbeat — toward the beat, the rhythm, the felt state in the chest — what was background can become foreground. The heart had been transmitting already. The difference is that the signal becomes more available to experience.

This is part of the architecture beneath I Feel.

The heart also participates in what the organism detects as emotionally significant. The body already knows this. It knows the sudden drop before bad news, the tightening before a difficult truth, the opening warmth when a room becomes safe, and the strange settling when something finally aligns.

The research does not create the experience. It gives us a way to respect what the organism has been reporting all along.

The heart is continuously participating in the organism's state through rhythm.

Not rate alone — rhythm.

Heart rate tells us how fast. Heart rate variability tells us something subtler: how flexibly the heart is adapting from beat to beat. A healthy heart is not a metronome. It varies. It listens. It responds. The spaces between beats carry information about stress, recovery, autonomic balance, emotional state, and the organism's capacity to adjust to what is happening.

Stress changes the rhythm. Grief changes it. Appreciation changes it. Genuine care changes it. The relationship is complex, and heart rhythm is not an emotional truth detector. The heart cannot be turned into a private lie detector, a spiritual scoreboard, or a machine for proving what a person 'really' feels.

But the coupling is relevant enough to examine.

Emotional state and cardiac rhythm are in conversation. The heart's rhythm reflects our emotional state. Our emotional state shapes the rhythm. The rhythm then becomes part of what the brain receives next.

The relationship runs both directions.

This is why the heart belongs in I Feel.

The heart responds to the real state of the body. It reports that state upward. The brain receives it. The rest of the body answers it. The rhythm becomes part of the weather the person is trying to navigate.

When the rhythm is more flexible and ordered, the body often has more room. Reflection may have more room. Connection may have more room. The space between signal and action may have more room. The head-brain receives a steadier stream from below, and the whole system may have a better chance of staying available to more than emergency.

When rhythm is jagged, stressed, or unstable, the body is reporting load. The field tightens. The head-brain receives the weather of the body as part of the problem it is trying to solve. Under those conditions, the space between signal and action can compress. Deliberation becomes harder to hold. I Will moves closer to I Do.

That is physiology with poetic consequences.

The chest tightens before the sentence is clear. The rhythm changes before the story has caught up. The body is already reporting something the head-brain will soon try to explain.

Sometimes the explanation will be accurate.

Often enough, it will be a story wrapped around a signal it barely heard.

The Compass asks attention to travel far enough to reach the signal before the explanation becomes the whole world.

The heart has been transmitting since before you were born.

The Compass gives that listening a language.

The Head Brain

The head-brain arrived late to the report.

This is easy to forget because it is so good at explaining everything afterward.

The head-brain's contributions are extraordinary: language, abstraction, memory, future simulation, planning, self-reflection, moral reasoning, symbolic meaning. The gut and heart cannot do what the head-brain does. The mistake is giving the head-brain sole authority over reports it did not originate.

Three patterns matter most for navigation.

The first is story.

When attention is not captured by an external task, the brain often turns toward memory, future simulation, self-reference, and social imagination. The Default Mode Network is one major neural correlate of this internally directed activity. It participates in the running account of who we are, what happened, what might happen, what others may think, and what this moment means.

This is the story machine doing one of its primary jobs.

A creature with memory and anticipation needs some thread connecting yesterday's wound, tomorrow's risk, and the present decision. Without that thread, identity in the ordinary sense would not hold. The story machine is a feature.

The problem begins when it intercepts and interprets the signal before the signal can be attended to as itself.

The gut and heart are already transmitting. The body's reports are already moving upward, already shaping baseline, affect, readiness, and salience. The story machine meets those signals quickly. Before the mind is fully aware of what the body has reported, the narrative has often begun assembling around it.

The sensation gets explained before it is attended to. The data gets processed into meaning before it has been allowed to surface as itself.

Sometimes the account is accurate. Often enough, it is incomplete.

The second pattern is threat.

The amygdala and related threat systems are optimized for survival speed. They link cues to defensive responses before the prefrontal cortex has time to form a considered response. We do not need perfect information to begin preparing for danger. We need enough information to survive the next second.

The survival advantage is obvious.

The cost for navigation is significant.

When the system detects what it reads as threat, the body begins preparing. Heart rate changes. Muscles ready. Attention narrows. We become more ready to act and less available to wonder.

This is excellent architecture for a predator. Or for prey.

It is more complicated in a marriage, a workplace, a classroom, a church meeting, a text thread, or a quiet kitchen where the threat signal is real in the body and uncertain in the world.

The amygdala is far from stupid. It is efficiently doing what fast threat systems do. It reads for danger under uncertainty. But it can mobilize around social danger, remembered danger, anticipated danger, or resemblance to danger with the urgency of physical threat. The body may begin acting as if survival is at stake before the person has had time to ask what is actually happening.

So far, the head-brain has given us two problems for navigation: story can explain the signal too quickly, and threat can move us to action before reflection catches up.

The third pattern is deliberation under load.

The prefrontal cortex helps make delay, context, inhibition, planning, and reflective choice available. Under lower load, the space between signal and action is easier to hold. The organism can consider more than the loudest signal.

Under high load, stress chemistry changes the balance. Prefrontal availability decreases. Habitual and defensive systems become more dominant. The space narrows.

I Will compresses toward I Do.

Instead of acting from deliberation we act from the signal. This is part of the neuroscience of a bio-loop without a Compass: story running, threat systems firing, deliberation narrowing, action gathering around urgency before the person can locate the need underneath it.

This is also where state matters.

Some nervous-system models describe a shift between social engagement, mobilization, and shutdown. Polyvagal theory gives one influential language for that pattern, though the details are debated and the Compass does not depend on every claim being settled. The useful point is narrower: the state of the nervous system shapes what capacities are available. Connection, reflection, curiosity, speech, learning, and deliberate choice are easier in some states than in others.

That is why the Compass becomes hardest to read precisely when it is most needed.

Under acute threat, chronic stress, exhaustion, trauma activation, shame, or overload, the capacities required to hold the Compass become less available. Attention narrows. Curiosity can collapse into closure. I Think becomes louder and less flexible. I Will becomes harder to find. I Need may be hidden beneath urgency. I Feel may remain as raw valence: bad, unsafe, too much, get away, make it stop.

This is not a design flaw.

It is survival architecture.

It is also why compassion matters when someone cannot find the bearing under load. The system has not become defective. It has returned to older capacities because older capacities are what it knows to reach when survival feels at stake.

The head-brain is not the enemy of navigation.

It is the most recently evolved participant in a system that was already spinning before it arrived. Its story machine is one of the Compass's greatest assets when we have enough capacity, and one of its greatest obstacles when the story closes too quickly. Its threat architecture can save a life, and it can mistake resemblance for reality. Its prefrontal capacities make possible the space between signal and action, and those capacities are vulnerable under load.

That is why the head must be read without being enthroned.

What the Compass Reads

Gut, heart, head: three embodied signal centers contributing simultaneously to what the bio-loop generates and what the Compass reads.

The gut is ancient chemistry below the threshold of awareness, shaping the baseline the whole organism is operating from. It tends toward Need — the body-level urgency that precedes any named feeling or conscious thought.

The heart is rhythmic, measurable, continuous. It tends toward Feel — the organism's affective report of its own state, carried in the felt quality of the chest and the rhythm of every beat.

The head-brain narrates, predicts, threat-detects, deliberates — and sometimes overwhelms the other two with the speed and volume of its own explanations. It tends toward Think — the story the mind constructs around what the body is already saying.

None of these tendencies are exclusive. The gut contributes to Feel. The heart contributes to Think. The head-brain contributes to Need through every narrative it constructs about what is required. All three are always contributing to all of it.

But the tendencies are real enough to help us navigate.

The instrument is calibrated for the whole organism.

One bearing for the ground that holds the storm.

One bearing for the head-brain's narrative function.

One bearing for the body-level urgency the gut tends toward.

One bearing for the affective signal the heart tends toward.

One bearing for the action the whole system drives toward when the bio-loop requires movement.

The head-brain is extraordinary. It is also late to the report.

The gut may be pressing before the need has a name. The heart may be signaling before the story has meaning. The head may be explaining before it has listened. We can learn to move attention far enough to read all three.

All three are sending.

All three are contributing.

All three can be read more honestly when the one holding the Compass is present enough to notice the reports before the story machine has explained them into something else.

That presence is not guaranteed. It is not automatic. It is not produced by knowing the names of the structures involved. Knowing what the Default Mode Network does will not quiet it. Knowing that stress weakens prefrontal availability does not restore it.

Knowledge is the head-brain's instrument, and the head-brain is only one participant in the storm.

What is needed here is prior to knowledge.

What is needed is ground.

Not the kind the head-brain constructs from its own conclusions. The kind that was present before the story machine came online. Before the signal had been interpreted. Before the head-brain had assembled an explanation for what the gut and heart were already reporting.

That ground is where the next chapter begins.

It is the only thing that makes the rest navigable.

The three-center account presented here is the working version — sufficient for navigation. The fuller biological detail, the research behind the gut-brain axis, and the wider literature on how each center contributes to the bio-loop's signal will be available at https://waynegwilliams.com/

CHAPTER 7 — I Am

The Compass's True North: the ground beneath the storm that makes the other bearings readable. Find it. Return to it. Find it again.

I Am.

It is assumed because it is.

The most ordinary thing you do is also one of the strangest things any organism has ever done.

You are aware that you exist.

You exist. So does a blue whale. So does an oak tree. So does the coffee plant, and the cup that holds what we brew from what the plant makes. Existence is everywhere. But you are aware of yours. You can notice and consider the fact of your own presence — that there is someone here to whom all of this is happening.

That is extraordinary.

The architecture required to support that noticing is almost impossible to overstate: neural complexity, memory, sensation, interoception, recursive self-modeling, language, attention, and the strange capacity to turn toward experience while experience is happening. The human organism does not merely have a bio-loop. It can notice that the loop is spinning. It can feel the storm and also recognize: this storm is happening to me.

Every living thing before us already had a spinning homeostatic loop. Need, signal, action. Faithful, continuous, alive. The bacterium moved toward what sustained it. The fish turned through water. The deer froze at the edge of the clearing. Life was already reading, reaching, correcting, surviving.

But in the human organism, something comes into focus with peculiar clarity.

The fish is in water. It may sense pressure, current, light, threat, direction. But it does not sit at the edge of the river wondering what it means to be a fish. The oak turns toward light without needing a story about light. The body knows a thousand things before the mind has a name for any of them.

And then, at some point in the long unfolding of life, the architecture became complex enough for the organism to turn toward itself.

Something became available.

I Am.

A lived fact before it is a theory. The capacity so ordinary, so continuous, so taken for granted that it disappears into the background of every other experience. We assume it because it is always there. We miss it for exactly the same reason.

The ground the Compass is held from is the presence you are already standing in. It may be hard to feel in the storm. It is always there to be found.

Someone is here. Noticing the weather. Holding the Compass. That is what I Am points toward. If the Compass has a True North, this is it.

I started noticing something years ago after attending a religious revival a friend was hosting. The preacher kept referring to Jesus as the “Great I Am” in a way I had not heard before. It was intentional. Evocative. Almost musical in the way she returned to it. The phrase struck a chord in me that resonated.

I am.

Two small words, so common they nearly disappear. I had said them thousands of times without hearing them. But that night the sentence would not close. It was complete, grammatically, and still it carried a pull, as if it wanted to lead somewhere.

I am... what?

At first, the phrase pointed toward the body. I am hungry. I am thirsty. I am tired.

Then it moved toward emotion. I am afraid. I am angry. I am sad. I am happy.

When I stayed with it longer, the field widened.

I am nervous. I am confused. I am curious. I am content. I am dissatisfied.

I noticed whatever could be present began stepping forward, one predicate at a time.

Then I began to hear how easily those predicates can harden into identity. I am lazy. I am depressed. I am broken. I am lost.

That was concerning. The phrase felt too powerful to be handled casually. A sentence that begins as location can become a verdict before we notice the turn.

So I went back to it, letting it play out. Letting it complete in as many ways as it needed to. Until it was all that was left.

Just: I Am.

And I left it there.

Incomplete.

Waiting.

What I found in that pause surprised me.

After the bodily sensations had named themselves, after the immediate emotions had risen and passed, after the wider field had spread out and settled, the pause narrowed back toward something more interior. A thought appeared with emotional weight behind it. Less like an ordinary thought and more like a warning. Something in me seemed to caution against lingering there.

But curiosity held.

So I stayed.

I did not argue with the thought. I did not correct it. I did not agree with it. I let it speak without interruption, without forcing, without building a defense against it.

Just listening.

Curiously.

Something I had been moving past for years finally had room to finish its sentence. I recognized it as mine. Not as the whole of me. Not as the truth about me. Mine, because it had been carried in me, asking to be heard.

That recognition was cathartic. Being with it without judgment or shame felt less like solving a problem and more like letting something exhausted finally sit down.

Then something quieter appeared underneath.

It was not insight. It was not a breakthrough in the usual sense. It was smaller than that. Simpler.

It's okay, I thought.

I am okay.

Then even that fell away.

Just:

I Am.

Say the sentence aloud, or only inside yourself, and let it sit.

I am.

Do you feel the pull?

It is complete, and still it wants a predicate. It tries to answer a question: I am... what? What am I?

Let it complete in as many ways as it needs to.

I am thirsty.

I am afraid.

I am a good person.

I am ashamed.

I am going to lose this.

I am trying.

Whatever comes, let it come. Let the predicates arrive. Let them finish. Let the body speak first if that is where it goes. Let the emotions follow. Let the story add its names. Let identity try to make its declarations.

Then see what remains when the predicates have spent themselves.

Just:

I Am.

Still here.

Before the Compass can be read. Before the other bearings can orient you, there is something that has to be present first.

You.

Not the version of you that is anxious, exhausted, ashamed, bracing, or caught inside the story about what happened. Something prior to all of that. Something that was present before this storm had a name and will be present after it passes.

That is I Am.

A recognition, not an affirmation. Not a declaration repeated until belief arrives. The simplest possible recognition: there is something here that is not the storm. Beneath the signal and the story and the noise, there is ground. You are the one the storm is moving through. You are not the storm itself.

Being somewhere and being present to it are not the same thing.

I Am is the difference.

This is where navigation begins. Before the Compass.

A compass in a tumbling hand points everywhere at once. The instrument is precise, but precision requires something stable enough to hold it. That stability does not have to be perfect. It does not have to be calm. It only has to be present — your presence, however shaky, with whatever distance is possible between you and the experience you are having.

A small but crucial gap between the weather and the one standing in it.

In that gap is I Am.

And once found, even briefly, even imperfectly, it changes how the rest of the storm is held.

Finding it is simple to describe and genuinely difficult to do, especially when the storm is loud. The bio-loop generates signals. The signals demand action. Urgency fills the room until it feels like there is no time to stop, no ground available to find, no space between the feeling and what the feeling requires right now.

That urgency is itself a signal.

It has a source.

It is pointing at something.

The first act of navigation is noticing that urgency can be observed without being obeyed immediately. It is happening in you, but it is not the whole of you. The part that notices the urgency is not itself urgent in the same way.

That is the opening.

But urgency is only one way the ground becomes hard to find. The bio-loop can also spin quiet. Not calm — dim. The colors slightly faded. The whole of experience arriving through gauze. No storm pressing urgently against you, just a flatness. A constant gray drizzle refusing to let any light in, making the search for ground feel like insurmountable terrain before it has even begun.

When there is little energy in the system, I Am does not feel lost so much as unavailable. Unreachable. Obscured. Eclipsed. The effort required to find it exceeds what is currently available.

Both storms obscure the ground.

The loud one and the dim one.

The Compass is difficult to read from either place.

I Am is a recognition. Like all genuine recognitions, once made, it cannot be unmade. Only forgotten. Then remembered. Lost, then found again.

The ground can be lost. This is worth saying plainly, because the loss rarely announces itself as loss. It registers instead as simply the way things are. As who you are. As the truth about you, finally revealed.

The signal that was supposed to be information becomes identity.

I am anxious.

I am broken.

I am someone who cannot handle this.

These are not reports anymore. They are the storm occupying the ground that was meant to hold it.

I Am is the first of the five sentences for a reason. It is the Compass's True North. It does not point at one domain of the bio-loop the same way as I Think, I Feel, I Need, and I Will / I Do.

It gives the other bearings an orienting point.

I Am makes the Compass readable.

— In Brief

I Am is the Compass's True North: the ground beneath the storm.

You are aware that you exist.

That presence — the one noticing the weather, holding the Compass — is the ground.

It was here before this storm. It will be here after.

Find it. Return to it. Find it again.

— Explored

The question philosophy kept circling back to, across centuries and languages and schools that agreed on almost nothing else, was this:

What is the thing that is aware of experience?

Not the content of awareness. Not the thought being thought, the feeling being felt, the image arriving through the eyes, the pressure in the chest, the sound entering the room. The question is about the one to whom all of it is arriving.

The subject that remains while the objects of experience change.

The "I" that was present when you were seven and is present now, reading this sentence, even though your body has changed, your beliefs have shifted, your circumstances have transformed, and the child you were could not have imagined the life now carrying their name.

What is that?

The Philosophers' Wall

Edmund Husserl, working in the early twentieth century, developed a method he called the *epoché* — a bracketing of assumptions about the external world so experience itself could be examined more carefully. When he looked there, he found that experience always has a basic shape: something is experienced, and something experiences it. Consciousness is always consciousness *of* something. But the consciousness itself

— the one to whom experience appears — never becomes an object in quite the same way. It is always there in the looking, always prior to the thing being looked at.

His student Martin Heidegger pushed the question in another direction. What he called *Dasein* — often translated as "being-there" — was his attempt to name the strange kind of being human beings have: not merely existing, but existing in a way that includes awareness of existence. The being for whom being is a question.

Heidegger noticed the trap. We cannot get behind ourselves to inspect ourselves like an object in a room. Any attempt to observe the observer is already another act of the observer. The one looking is already there before the looking begins.

William James, working from yet another direction, made a similar distinction between the "I" and the "me." The "me" is everything that can be made into an object of reflection: my body, my history, my personality, my roles, my story. The "I" is the one doing the reflecting.

And the "I" has a strange property.

It never appears in its own visual field.

You can think about yourself, but the you doing the thinking is not the same as the you being thought about. The knower slips away the moment you try to make it the known.

Three philosophers.

Three different doorways.

The same wall.

The Contemplatives' Door

The contemplative traditions arrived at the same wall through a different door.

They were not, for the most part, trying to solve a philosophical problem. They were trying to address suffering. Not suffering as an idea, but suffering as weather: fear that would not quiet, craving that would not release, grief that would not finish, thought that kept circling the same wound until the person carrying it could no longer tell the wound from the self.

So they sat.

They prayed.

They fasted.

They watched the breath, crossed deserts, entered monasteries, chanted through the night, knelt beside beds, walked in silence, stayed with pain long enough for the first explanations to exhaust themselves.

And again and again, across traditions that disagreed about almost everything else, a similar report returned.

Beneath the suffering, there was something that was not suffering.

Something the suffering was happening to.

Something that remained when the storm was no longer being mistaken for the whole sky.

The Vedic traditions spoke of *Atman* — the self beneath body, mind, emotion, and story. The witness. The one not finally reducible to the changing contents of experience.

Christian mystics spoke of the soul, though often with more depth than the ordinary use of the word suggests: the innermost place where the human person could be met by God, prior to performance, prior to explanation, prior to the constructed self trying to secure its own existence.

Buddhist traditions, careful about turning experience into a permanent self, spoke instead of awareness, Buddha-nature, emptiness, or the luminous quality of mind — not as a possession to defend, but as the open field in which grasping could be seen, loosened, and released.

The Sufis spoke of the heart, though not merely the organ beating in the chest. The heart as the innermost center. The place where divine nearness could be received when the noise of the nafs — the grasping, defensive, self-protective ego — grew quiet enough for something deeper to be heard.

Different names.

Different maps.

Different prayers.

Different warnings about what should and should not be concluded from what is found there.

But the report keeps returning: there is a depth beneath the constructed self. A presence beneath the storm. A stillness that does not feel manufactured by the quiet, but revealed when the noise stops claiming the whole field.

This convergence is worth honoring carefully.

The traditions did not agree on what the ground ultimately is. They did not agree on God, self, soul, emptiness, creation, liberation, union, or final reality. Their interpretations diverged, sometimes radically. But their practitioners kept finding a recognizable shape in experience: the storm is not the whole of what we are. Something remains available beneath it, or behind it, or within it, depending on the language each tradition trusted.

That does not prove a single metaphysical conclusion.

It does suggest that the ground is not an invention of this instrument.

The Compass did not create I Am. It gives a plain name to something human beings have been finding, losing, remembering, and returning to for as long as they have taken the storm seriously enough to sit still inside it.

Where the Compass Stops

Here the inquiry reaches its edge.

Philosophy can describe the structure. It can notice that the observer never fully becomes the observed, that the subject slips away when we try to make it an object, that awareness seems to be the condition in which experience appears rather than just another piece of experience.

The contemplative traditions can carry us deeper into the felt terrain. They can teach practices for quieting the storm, loosening identification, and returning to the ground beneath the weather. They can report, with centuries of disciplined witness behind them, that something remains when thought, fear, craving, and story have lost their grip.

But what that ground ultimately is remains beyond what the Compass can settle.

Is awareness produced by the brain — an emergent property of sufficient biological complexity, inseparable from the machinery that makes it possible?

Is it prior to the brain — something the body receives, expresses, localizes, or carries without originating?

Is it the soul, the witness, the image of God, Buddha-nature, Atman, presence, consciousness, or some reality our available words keep circling without capturing?

The answers diverge.

The finding does not.

Again and again, human beings report the same practical discovery: experience changes when the storm is no longer mistaken for the whole self. Something can stand beneath the weather. Something can notice the falling apart without being identical to the falling. Something can hold the signal, the story, the need, and the action without collapsing into any one of them.

That is where the Compass is allowed to speak.

It cannot tell us what the ground is made of.

It can tell us that the ground is findable.

It cannot resolve whether awareness is ultimate or emergent, received or created, divine or biological, or some mystery that makes those divisions too small.

It can tell us that finding I Am gives the other bearings somewhere to orient from.

The ground cannot ground itself. The eye cannot step outside seeing to inspect the condition that makes sight possible. The one who asks what am I? is already present inside the asking. Every attempt to get behind awareness happens within awareness.

That is not a flaw in the inquiry. It is the shape of the territory.

The Compass stops where ontology begins to outrun navigation. It does not need to decide what the ground ultimately is in order to help you find it. It only needs to point toward the lived fact that something is here, aware that the storm is happening, and not exhausted by the storm.

That is enough for the work this instrument is built to do.

The rest belongs to deeper waters.

What Navigation Requires

For navigation, the question does not have to be resolved.

The Compass is a practical instrument. It locates. It orients. It makes legible what the storm's noise would otherwise obscure. And what I Am locates — the ground beneath the weather, the presence the storm moves through, the you who was here before this particular difficulty began and will be here after it passes — can be found without settling what that ground ultimately is.

You do not need to know whether awareness is produced by the brain or prior to it in order to find the part of you that is not the anxiety. You do not need a settled position on the soul's origins to notice that something in you is witnessing the falling apart and is not itself falling. You do not need to resolve twenty-five centuries of philosophical and theological dispute to take a breath, find the ground, and read the Compass.

The ground is present.

Finding it gives the Compass its orienting point.

That is enough for navigation.

For some, the finding will feel like more than a useful feature of experience. It may feel like a clue worth following. The

Compass can point to its edge. What lies beyond it belongs to a different instrument.

The Compass orients within the storm. A lighthouse reveals where the storm sits within something larger. That is a different instrument, and it belongs to a different inquiry.

Here, the Compass can say this honestly:

The ground is real enough to stand on.

It is findable.

It holds.

And whatever it ultimately is, it has been with you through every storm. It will be with you through the next one.

The wood still needs chopping. The water still needs carrying. Tuesday is still Tuesday, and the storm is still the storm.

But the storm is not the whole of what you are.

You are the one standing in it.

That is not a small thing.

That is, in fact, everything.

PART THREE: THE COMPASS

CHAPTER 8 — I Think

I Think — The story the mind is telling right now. Let it finish. Notice that it is a story. Sit in the pause long enough for the right question to arrive. Ask whether it is true only when there is enough ground to ask honestly.

I was sitting in a windowless conference room, the air thick with stale coffee and the hum of a ventilation system that could not quite keep up. Across from me was my supervisor. Between us was a stack of case files that represented human lives in various stages of unraveling.

My gut had been churning for weeks — slow, acidic, indifferent to my career trajectory. My heart had been carrying a hollow, fluttering ache in my chest, unable to reconcile the chasm between the help that was needed and the help I was able to provide.

But my head-brain was busy building a masterpiece of obfuscation.

It was acting as my defense attorney, and it knew exactly which arguments I would believe.

You're just tired, it argued. *If you quit now, you're failing these kids. You've put years into this. You can't walk away without a better plan. Just keep your head down and do the work. You're fine. This is just part of the job.*

In that room, after my supervisor assigned me three more cases, apologized for the turnover, and left, I was sitting in the collision of two different kinds of truth.

First, there was the truth that did not need my permission. My nervous system was in chronic mobilization. The human organism has limits, and I had exceeded mine months before. Whether I believed I was strong enough did not matter. The physics of burnout are as unforgiving as the physics of gravity. Some stories are true whether you want to believe them or not.

Second, there was the story that wanted to be true.

You are failing these kids if you leave.

That story was not random. It was not stupid. It had evidence. It had moral force. It wore the clothes of compassion. It let me keep believing that what was happening to me was sacrifice instead of collapse.

But my gut knew the story was not honest. My heart knew it too. An exhausted, hollowed-out version of me was not helping anyone. The head-brain can take a terrifying reality — *I am breaking* — and reframe it. It can look at spiritual death and call it noble sacrifice.

Some stories are not true no matter how badly you want them to be.

And then there are the stories that become true in their consequences because you have believed them long enough.

I am a person who does not complete things.

That was one of mine.

The evidence was real. Projects started and abandoned. A hardbound journal with eighteen pages of heartfelt commitment to self-reflection, followed by blank paper. The six credits missing from the high school diploma that should have had my name on it.

The story machine took that evidence and built an identity from it.

This is who I am.

Then, because the story was running beneath every new beginning, it began generating evidence to confirm itself. The project that might have been finished was not, because finishing felt inconsistent with who I had become in the story. The degree was not completed, again, for the same invisible reason.

The story became architecture.

The architecture generated its own proof.

The gut kept signaling capacity. The heart kept broadcasting the specific grief of unlived potential. The head-brain kept explaining both away with the story it had already decided was true.

The signal center in your head is the only one that can narrate falsely about itself. The heart cannot tell itself it is calm while it is racing. The gut cannot talk itself into being settled while it is in knots. They report the weather. Only the head can look at a hurricane and try to convince you it is a light breeze.

This is not a criticism.

It is an extraordinary capacity — the ability to take the raw, continuous flow of experience and shape it into coherence. Into sequence, causation, meaning. Into a line that connects what happened yesterday to what is happening now to what might happen tomorrow. Into a world that makes enough sense to move through.

The head-brain tells stories because stories help us live.

They help us remember, predict, prepare, explain, belong, endure, and hope. They let a creature with memory and anticipation carry a life across time.

There is a story.

There is always a story.

That is not the problem.

The problem begins when the story disappears as story and starts presenting itself as the world.

The bearing I Think is just this: noticing the story.

Just — *oh.*

There is a story here.

The mind is doing the thing it does.

There is a narrator, and there is a narration, and for this moment I can feel the difference between the two.

The storyteller is not the story.

That moment of distinction, however brief and however hard won, is the beginning. When the narrator and the narration are no longer fused, a small opening appears.

In that opening is also I Am.

When the gap goes unnoticed, when no one is watching the story machine, it runs. And runs. And runs. Somewhere along the way it stops feeling like a story and starts feeling like the truth. The facts. The way things are. The way you are. The way things are going to stay.

The narrator disappears into the narration.

And you are no longer reading the story.

You are living inside it.

Inside the room built from your own conclusions.

It is a convincing room. It is built from real things — real experiences, real pain, real patterns the story machine identified and pieced together carefully. It does not feel like a cage. It feels like clarity.

When truth stops being questioned, that is often the signal that the room has closed.

Some of the conclusions may be accurate. Some of the patterns may be real patterns worth taking seriously. But an accurate pattern is not the same as a permanent truth.

A pattern observed is not a destiny confirmed.

That I had not completed some things was true. That I was a person who does not complete things was a room.

The story machine, operating without the ground of I Am beneath it, cannot always tell the difference.

Without the ground, every conclusion feels final.

But the story did not build the room out of malice.

It built it because a room can feel safer than weather. A conclusion, even a painful one, can be easier to live inside than the terrifying openness of not knowing.

I am someone who does not finish things may protect a person from the risk of trying again.

I am unlovable may protect someone from the vulnerability of reaching.

Nothing ever changes may protect someone from the pain of hope returning too soon.

Some rooms were shelters before they became cages.

And not every story begins alone.

Some stories are built in relationship and carried privately for years. Some are carried communally for generations. A child learns what can be said, what must not be needed, what kind of person they are, what kind of world they live in, from the faces and silences and repeated conclusions around them long before they know they are receiving a story.

We are loop-first creatures, but we live story-first.

The bio-loop moves first — need, signal, action — but we experience that movement through the story the head-brain builds around it. What this feeling means. What this pattern proves. What kind of person I am. What kind of world this is. What can be hoped for. What must never be risked again.

And we have never lived inside a greater abundance of stories than we do now.

At the swipe of a thumb, the story machine can borrow a thousand explanations for the same signal. Some liberate. Some clarify. Some name what had been nameless for years. Others harden too quickly, offering identity where orientation was needed, certainty where curiosity was still required, tribe where truth had not yet been examined.

A grounded mind can hold a story as a map: useful, partial, revisable.

A frightened mind may need the story to become a room.

A shamed mind may turn it into a verdict.

A lonely mind may turn it into belonging.

That is why the pause matters.

The first task is not to defeat the story. It is to stay with it long enough for the proper question to surface.

This is where humility becomes useful in its truest sense. Humility is not self-erasure. It is the courage to let the story remain answerable to reality. A painful story can harden into identity, but so can a flattering one. *I am broken* can occupy the ground. So can *I am right.* So can *I am the one who sees clearly.* The emotional tone is different, but the danger is the same: the story becomes unavailable to correction.

The pause keeps the room open. It lets confidence remain teachable, pain remain question-bearing, and certainty remain honest enough to listen.

Is this true? may be the question.

Or: *What has this story been protecting?*

Or: *Was this story handed to me before I knew it was a story?*

Or: *How long has my family been carrying it?*

Or: *What need has been hidden underneath it?*

The right question may be more difficult to reach than the right answer, and more important.

A good therapy room often works because another person can hold the pause with you, listening for the question you are not yet able to ask alone. The Compass is not that full container. But it can create a smaller one: enough space for the story to finish speaking, enough ground to keep from being swallowed by it, enough curiosity for the question that wants to be asked to finally arrive.

A story can be true, false, partial, protective, borrowed, inherited, communal, outdated, or newly useful.

Before any of that can be known, it has to become visible as story.

That is what I Think asks.

The first move is visibility. Before replacement, before argument, before correction, the story has to be seen.

What story is running right now?

Later, if there is enough ground, you can ask whether it is true.

Later still, if there is enough curiosity, you can ask what it has been protecting.

But first, notice the story as a story.

One thing worth knowing about this bearing before you reach for it: under load, the story machine can get louder.

Faster.

More certain.

Less examined.

The capacity to notice the story as story — to hold it at enough distance for the right question to rise — compresses when the signal is running hot. Not because you have failed. Because the ground required to examine the story is harder to find when the storm is loud.

When I Think is running loudest and examining least, that is not failure.

That is the Compass reporting accurately on the conditions that exist.

Work with what is here.

A fragment of ground. A single breath. The smallest possible gap between the narrator and the narration. A question not yet ready to be answered, but finally allowed to arrive.

That may be enough — not enough to solve the whole story. Enough to stop living entirely inside it.

— In Brief

The head-brain tells stories. It has to.

I Think is the bearing that notices the story has arrived.

When the story becomes visible, the pause opens. In that pause, the right question can arise.

Is this true?

What has this story been protecting?

Was this story handed to me before I knew it was a story?

What need has been hidden underneath it?

Notice the story first.

The questions come after.

That is often enough to keep I Am from being occupied by the room the story built.

— Explored

I Think is the Compass bearing that makes the story visible.

The head-brain does not wait for reality to finish arriving before it begins explaining it. It receives signal, sensation, memory, expectation, social context, and threat assessment all at once, and it begins assembling a usable account before conscious awareness has caught up. By the time a thought appears as *what I think*, much of the work has already happened underneath it.

This is why story feels so immediate.

It does not usually arrive as speculation. It arrives as recognition. The mind does not say, *Here is one possible interpretation of the signal currently moving through the organism.* It says, *This is what is happening. This is what it means. This is who I am. This is what comes next.*

That speed is useful. A human being could not move through the world if every sensation had to be examined from the beginning each time. The story machine compresses complexity into something livable. It lets the past teach, the future be rehearsed, danger be anticipated, relationships be interpreted, and identity hold across time.

But the same capacity that makes life coherent can also make the wrong coherence feel like truth.

A story can organize pain so well that the pain finally seems to make sense. It can make disappointment predictable. It can turn chaos into a room with walls. It can give a child an explanation for what should never have needed explaining. It can let a family survive what no one was allowed to name. It can carry a community's warning long after the original danger has passed.

That is why stories are not merely private thoughts. Some are built in the mind. Some are built between people. Some are inherited as atmosphere before they are ever spoken as belief. By the time a person thinks, *this is just who I am*, the story may have already lived in faces, silences, expectations, warnings, jokes, prayers, punishments, family rules, cultural scripts, and inherited grief.

The head-brain may be narrating now, but it is often narrating with old material.

And it is not working with words alone.

The material it narrates with is arriving from everywhere. The gut's pressure. The heart's rhythm. The breath's pattern. The posture already bracing before the thought has formed. The old autonomic calibration that decides, before language, whether this room is safe enough to soften in.

The story machine has an organism underneath it.

That means a story is rarely just an idea. It is often the head-brain's translation of a larger field: tension, rhythm, expectation, readiness, recoil, hunger, numbness, pain, reach, remembered danger, inherited warning. The source may not be immediately clear. It may not need to be clear at first. What matters is that the story is not arriving from nowhere.

This is why the question *is this true?* matters — and why it is sometimes not the first question that can be asked.

A story may be inaccurate and still have protected something real. It may be outdated and still once have been wise. It may be inherited and still feel personal. It may be false as a description of the present and faithful as a record of what the organism once had to survive.

I Think does not begin by putting the story on trial.

It begins by making the story visible enough to approach.

Once visible, the story can be studied without being obeyed. Its truth can be questioned. Its function can be honored. Its origin can be traced. Its cost can be measured. The need beneath it can begin to appear.

The pause matters because the first question is not always the right question.

Sometimes the right question is *is this true?*

Sometimes it is *what has this story been protecting?*

Sometimes it is *where did this story begin?*

Sometimes it is *what signal has this story been translating all this time?*

The right question does not arrive by force. It arrives when the story is given enough room to finish speaking and the whole organism is given enough room to answer.

The bearing begins there: with the machinery by which the head-brain turns signal into story, story into truth, truth into identity, and identity into a room that may once have sheltered the organism — and may now be ready to open.

The Brain's Best Guess

The word *prediction* is worth pausing on, because it names what the head-brain is doing before the story ever becomes a sentence.

The brain does not passively receive experience and then construct a narrative about it afterward. It is already generating predictions — constantly, automatically, beneath conscious awareness — about what is happening, what is likely to happen next, what matters, what can be ignored, what requires response.

Incoming sensory data does not arrive into an empty room. It arrives into expectation.

The brain is always making a model of the world and comparing that model against what the senses report. What we experience as perception is not the raw feed from the senses. It is the brain's best current guess about what is out there, updated when incoming evidence forces the model to revise.

This is more than conjecture. It is architecture. Karl Friston's work on predictive processing describes a brain fundamentally in the business of reducing uncertainty — generating models of the world, testing them against evidence, and updating when the evidence demands revision. The story machine is functional. It helps the organism move through an uncertain world without being overwhelmed by undifferentiated data.

But the guess is never made by the head-brain alone.

The model is built from the whole organism's report: gut pressure, heart rhythm, breath, posture, memory, threat calibration, relational expectation, fatigue, hunger, pain, longing, shame, and the accumulated residue of what has happened before. The head-brain may narrate the guess, but the material it uses has been arriving from everywhere.

That is why the story can feel so true before it has been examined.

It is not floating above the body as an abstract thought. It is wearing the body's evidence. The tight chest, the dropped stomach, the accelerated pulse, the braced shoulders, the familiar dread — all of it can make the story feel less like an interpretation and more like recognition.

When the system works well, predictions are held lightly. Evidence that contradicts the model triggers an update. The story revises. The narrative stays flexible, responsive, alive to new information. This is I Think functioning as designed: the capacity to generate a working model and then let the model be wrong.

A mind that can let its model be wrong is a mind still capable of learning.

The difficulty begins when the prediction has been protecting something. When the story is not merely an estimate of reality, but a shelter built around pain, shame, danger, or need. Then contradiction does not feel like new information. It feels like threat. The evidence that might update the model feels like it might tear down the room the organism has been using to survive.

This is why the pause cannot be rushed.

The head-brain needs time to notice that its best guess is a guess. The body needs time to report more than the loudest signal. The story needs time to show whether it is describing the present, repeating the past, protecting an old wound, or carrying something handed down before it was ever chosen.

In that pause, the model can soften.

The story can become visible as story.

And the first honest question can begin to rise.

When Thought Becomes Truth

The pause is where a prediction can remain a prediction.

When the pause opens, the brain's best guess has room to stay flexible. The story can be tested, softened, revised, complicated, or allowed to remain unfinished. New information can enter. The body can report more than the loudest signal. The room has windows.

When the pause is unavailable, something else happens.

The guess hardens.

The story stops feeling like one possible account of reality and starts feeling like reality itself.

This is what clinical research calls **cognitive fusion** — the state in which thought is no longer experienced as thought, but as the world. Steven Hayes, who developed Acceptance and Commitment Therapy, built an entire clinical framework around this distinction. What ACT calls **defusion** is the movement from *I am unlovable* to *I am having the thought that I am unlovable.*

The content has barely changed.

The relationship to it has changed completely.

That shift matters because a fused thought cannot be examined from inside the fusion. It can only be obeyed, defended, lived inside, or fought against as if it were an external fact. The mind does not say, *I am telling a painful story about being unlovable.* It says, *I am unlovable.*

The story disappears into the surface of reality.

Once that happens, evidence stops arriving cleanly. A kind look becomes pity. Silence becomes rejection. Delay becomes abandonment. A mistake becomes proof. Success becomes an exception that does not count. The story does not need to invent all the evidence. Much of the evidence may be real. Fusion changes what the evidence is allowed to mean.

This is the danger of thought becoming truth.

A flexible story can learn.

A fused story can only confirm.

The head-brain is still doing its job: reducing uncertainty, preserving coherence, protecting the organism from surprise. Under enough load, that protection can become rigid. Surprise feels dangerous. Revision feels like exposure. The possibility that the story might be wrong can feel less like freedom and more like collapse.

That is why I Think begins with visibility.

The thought does not have to disappear.

The person does not have to win an argument against it.

A small grammatical space can open: *I am having the thought that...*

In that space, the story remains present, but it is no longer the whole world. It can be held. It can be questioned. It can be listened to. It can be tested against what the body is reporting, what the situation actually contains, and what the story may have failed to see.

The pause returns.

And with the pause, the possibility of the next honest question.

That is where I Think begins to do its work: not by proving the story false, but by letting it become visible enough that truth can approach it.

The Grammar of Identity

The grammatical shift is not incidental. It is structural.

Listen to the way we talk about ourselves.

I am anxious.

I am depressed.

I am angry.

I am not enough.

We reach for these constructions without thinking. In conversation. In the privacy of the mind. In the texts we send and the journals we keep. The sentence is ordinary enough to pass unnoticed, but it is doing enormous work. It takes the weather moving through the organism and gives it the grammar of identity.

The storm receives the name of the ground.

Ludwig Wittgenstein wrote that the limits of my language are the limits of my world. The insight is not merely literary. Language does not only describe what we see. It helps determine what can be seen, what can be thought, what can be distinguished, what can be acted on. The structure of a sentence can become the structure of a world.

That matters most in the sentences we use before we have finished understanding what they are carrying.

I am angry is not a neutral report. It places the signal inside the self. Anger may be the bio-loop doing its job — pointing at violation, obstruction, danger, grief, exhaustion, or need. But the sentence does not leave it there. It does not say anger is moving through me. It says I am angered into identity. It lets the weather occupy the ground.

There are other ways to say it.

I feel angry.

There is anger present.

I notice anger moving through me.

These are not euphemisms. They are structurally different claims. They preserve the difference between the ground and the signal, between the one having the experience and the experience being had, between I Am and I Feel.

This is not a prescription for precious language. No one needs to police every sentence, correct every casual phrase, or turn ordinary speech into a technical exercise. The point is simpler and more serious: the story machine uses grammar automatically. It does this below the level of conscious choice, thousands of times across the ordinary days of an ordinary life. It places signal into identity, interpretation into reality, weather into ground.

The collapse rarely begins dramatically. It begins in small grammatical surrenders, each one rehearsing fusion a little further. A feeling becomes a self-description. A pattern becomes a trait. A wound becomes a name. A conclusion becomes the room from which everything else is interpreted.

Then the story machine does what it always does.

It builds.

When I Am is stable, thought has somewhere to stand without becoming the ground itself. The story can be useful, provisional, revisable. It can say, *I think this is happening*, and the trailing *I think* keeps the room open.

When I Am is lost — when the self has fused with the signal, when the storm has occupied the ground — the story machine still needs an anchor. The bio-loop requires narrative function. The mind still has to organize experience into something coherent enough to move through. So the story machine finds the next available structure.

It builds on itself.

Descartes gave us the famous line: *I think, therefore I am.* His aim was to find the one thing that could not be doubted, the fixed point from which everything else could be reconstructed. If thinking is happening, something must be doing the thinking. The thinker is inferred from the thought.

The degradation sequence is the dark inversion of that sentence.

Not *I think, therefore I am.*

I am what I think I am, I think.

The self collapses into its own narration. The story generates the self that generates the story that confirms the self. Recursive. Reinforcing. Reductive. Each cycle tends to compress rather than expand, to simplify rather than complicate, to move toward the single verdict the system under stress can most easily hold.

The story becomes the storyteller.

The narration becomes the narrator.

And the self, needing ground and unable to find it, builds a room out of its own conclusions and moves in.

The Room

This room feels familiar.

You may be in it now, or you may have been in it recently enough to remember its walls. It rarely announces itself as crisis, collapse, or loss of Compass. It announces itself as clarity. As finally understanding. As seeing things as they really are, without the illusions that used to soften the truth.

The certainty that you are fundamentally unlovable — and that the evidence is too extensive to question honestly.

The knowledge that things do not work out for people like you — not as a pessimistic prediction, but as an observed pattern.

The conclusion that what happened means exactly what the story says it means, and that the story has been running long enough, confirmed often enough, that it no longer feels like a story.

It feels like the truth.

The room is built from real materials. Real experiences. Real pain. Real patterns the story machine identified accurately. That is what makes it so convincing. A room built from nothing would be easier to leave. This one has receipts. It has memory in the walls. It has names, dates, faces, losses, disappointments, warnings. It can point to what happened and say, *See?*

The problem is not the materials.

The problem is that the room has no windows.

The story machine, operating without the ground of I Am, has no reliable way to distinguish between *this is a pattern I have observed* and *this is the permanent truth about the nature of things.* Without ground, every conclusion feels final. Every pattern feels like destiny. Every story feels like territory rather than map.

And the room may have been useful once.

Some rooms were shelters before they became cages. Some conclusions kept a child from hoping too loudly in a house where hope was punished. Some kept a person from reaching toward people who had already proven unsafe. Some gave pain a reason when randomness would have been unbearable.

A story can be wrong about the present and still faithful to what the organism once had to survive.

That is why the bearing does not begin by smashing the walls.

It begins by noticing them.

What story is running right now?

What conclusion has the room been built around?

What does the room let me avoid feeling?

What does it protect me from risking?

What would become visible if one window opened?

These questions matter because the room is not only private. Some rooms are built in relationship and carried alone for years. Some are built by families, communities, religions, cultures, and histories, then handed down as atmosphere before anyone knows they are breathing it. The head-brain may be narrating now, but some of the room's materials were gathered long before the person had a choice about what to build with.

I Think does not ask the person to deny the room.

It asks them to find the edge of it.

The edge may be small at first. A flicker of doubt. A sentence that changes by one word.

I am unlovable becomes *I feel unlovable*, and then, when there is enough room, *I am having the thought that I am unlovable.*

Nothing changes becomes *nothing seems to change*, and then *something in me believes nothing changes.*

This is who I am becomes *this is the story I have been living inside.*

That shift may look small from the outside.

Inside the room, it is a window.

The story remains present. The walls do not vanish. The evidence does not disappear. But light enters. Air enters. The story can finally be seen as something constructed, something held, something that may have served and may now be costing more than it protects.

An open question can be moved through.

A closed room can only be inhabited.

Humility and the Open Question

This is where an old word becomes useful again.

Humility has often been misunderstood as self-reduction. As the refusal to take joy in what is good. As lowering the voice when delight rises too brightly. As pretending an accomplishment does not matter because acknowledging it might sound too close to pride.

That is not humility.

A person who has done something difficult and feels the clean surge of completion is not failing humility. A child who runs into the room holding the drawing they are proud of is not morally compromised by the brightness in their face. A worker who knows the task was done well, a parent who sees the fruit of long patience, a friend who says, with honest gladness, *I did that* — these are truthful recognitions of what has happened.

The problem is not the joy.

The problem is the story hardening around the self until correction can no longer enter.

Pride, in the dangerous sense, is not confidence. It is not delight. It is not the honest pleasure of seeing something true and good come through one's own effort. Pride is the self becoming unavailable to correction. The story closes around itself so tightly that no new evidence can enter.

Pride can harden in more than one direction.

Sometimes the story says, *I am nothing.*

Sometimes it says, *I am the only one who sees.*

Sometimes it says, *I am beyond correction.*

The emotional tone is different, but the structure is the same: the story has fused with identity so completely that questioning it feels like a threat to the self.

That is why pride is dangerous. Confidence can listen. Delight can receive. Accomplishment can remain grateful. Pride cannot remain in conversation with reality. Correction feels like humiliation. Apology feels like annihilation. Another person's truth feels like an attack. New evidence cannot enter without the room shaking.

Humility keeps the windows open.

Humility is not the opposite of confidence. It is the condition that keeps confidence correctable.

It lets achievement remain grateful. It lets conviction remain teachable. It lets strength remain relational. It allows a person to say, *I may be right,* without needing reality to stop speaking.

Meekness begins to recover its proper force here.

Meekness is not weakness. It is not passivity, compliance, or the loss of spine. It is strength under governance. Power that does not need to prove itself by hardening. A mind strong enough to remain open. A self grounded enough to be corrected. A body capable of standing in uncertainty without reaching too quickly for the safety of a final verdict.

I Think requires that kind of courage.

The story may be true. It may be partly true. It may have protected something real. It may have been handed down by people who needed it to survive. Humility lets the story remain a story long enough for the next honest question to arrive.

And sometimes that is the bravest thing a person can do.

When Stillness Becomes Threat

For some, the instruction to pause and notice the story is not simple.

It is intolerable.

Marcus Raichle's research on the Default Mode Network revealed what happens in the brain between tasks — when external demands pause and the mind is left to itself. What he found was not rest in the ordinary sense. The so-called resting brain is active: reviewing the past, modeling the future, maintaining the thread of self that holds a life together across time.

The unoccupied mind has a destination.

And that destination is not neutral.

It is shaped by what the story machine has accumulated.

Bruce McEwen's research on allostatic load helps name what accumulates. Acute stress is the single demand, the immediate threat, the challenge the system was designed to meet and then discharge. Accumulated load is different. It is what happens when the demands keep arriving faster than the organism can metabolize them, when the baseline itself shifts upward, when what was meant to be temporary becomes the climate.

When the mind is no longer occupied by task, demand, noise, or stimulation, it often returns to what the organism has been carrying.

That return can feel dangerous.

For some, the danger arrives as productivity panic. Stillness feels like failure. Like laziness. Like falling behind. Like proof that nothing is being accomplished, nothing is improving, nothing is being earned. The story machine has learned to equate motion with worth, usefulness with safety, contribution with permission to exist. To stop moving is not rest. It is exposure.

For others, the danger arrives as deprivation. The screen goes quiet. The room goes still. The next hit of novelty does not arrive. Nothing is interrupting the mind quickly enough to keep it from returning to itself. The agitation rises almost immediately — not because the person is shallow or undisciplined, but because stimulation has been serving as a buffer between awareness and the stories waiting underneath it.

In both cases, the root may be the same.

The pause removes the cover.

What comes forward is the unoccupied mind's accumulated material: unfinished grief, shame, dread, resentment, loneliness, inherited warning, old verdicts, unnamed need, the running commentary that has been held at bay by motion or noise or the next thing.

For the person whose accumulated material is difficult but survivable, the instruction to observe the story may feel like an invitation. Uncomfortable, perhaps. But possible.

For the person whose story machine runs toward aversive territory the moment occupation ceases — whose default narrative overwhelms rather than informs — the instruction is not an invitation.

It is a threat.

This is why some people cannot sit still. Cannot let the mind idle. Cannot tolerate the gap between one task and the next without reaching for work, noise, the phone, the argument, the errand, the project, the next thing that keeps the story machine occupied with something other than where it wants to go.

The reaching is not a failure of discipline.

It is protection.

The bio-loop has learned that the unoccupied mind is unsafe, and it is protecting the organism the only way it knows how.

If this is your territory — if pausing to observe the story feels less like an opening and more like a door you cannot afford to walk through — the Compass is not asking you to force your way in. It is asking only that you know the door is there. That the story running is a story. That stillness may need to arrive in smaller doses, with more support, with more ground, and with more respect for what the pause has been threatening to reveal.

The bearing remains.

The instruction adjusts to what is actually possible.

Sometimes I Think begins with a question.

Sometimes it begins with noticing why the question cannot yet be asked.

An Opening

This is what I Think offers when the ground holds and the bearing is readable: the capacity to hold the story lightly enough to remember that it is a story.

That does not make the story false. It makes the story available.

Available to be questioned. Available to be listened to. Available to be traced back toward its source. Available to be honored for what it once protected and examined for what it now costs.

The story machine is working from incomplete information under changing conditions. It is building from signal, memory, prediction, pain, longing, threat, family weather, inherited warning, and whatever evidence the organism has been able to gather. Its conclusions may feel certain. Some may even be accurate. But certainty and accuracy are not the same as finality.

The trailing *I think* belongs at the end of every conclusion the mind reaches about who you are and what is possible for you.

I am unlovable, I think.

Nothing changes, I think.

This is who I am, I think.

That small phrase does not solve the story. It does not erase the evidence. It does not make pain imaginary or history irrelevant.

It opens a window.

It lets the room become a room again instead of the whole world.

From there, the next question can arrive.

Maybe: *Is this true?*

Maybe: *What has this story been protecting?*

Maybe: *What need has been waiting underneath it?*

The right question is not always the easiest one. It may not be the first one. It may need ground, time, support, and enough quiet for us to answer. But when it comes, it changes the room. It gives the bio-loop a better path than confirmation. It gives the story something more honest to do than keep proving itself.

Provisionality is not weakness. It is the mind's greatest strength when the ground is present to make it safe.

To hold a story as provisional is not to live without meaning. It is to live inside the best available meaning while remaining open to revision. It is to let the past teach without letting it imprison. To let pain speak without letting it name you. To let inherited stories be examined before they become destiny.

I Think does not ask the story machine to go silent.

It asks the storyteller to become visible.

And when the storyteller becomes visible, the story can finally become workable.

The room may still be there.

The walls may still be close.

But somewhere, even if only by a sentence, a window has opened.

That can be enough for the next bearing to become possible.

The treatment of I Think here is navigational — the story machine named precisely enough to work with. The fuller account of predictive processing, the neuroscience of narrative and the Default Mode Network, and the research literature on how language shapes experience will be available at
https://waynegwilliams.com/

CHAPTER 9 — I Feel

I Feel — The signal the body is sending right now, continually. Turn toward it. Let it be signal before it becomes explanation. Ask not how — ask what.

It was three in the morning somewhere outside Laramie, and the only world that existed was the fifty feet of pavement my headlights could reach.

Snow moved through the beams in bright, frantic streaks. The diesel was a steady hum in the floorboards, a vibration I had stopped noticing hours before. The cab was dark except for the instrument panel, the road, and the small circle of visibility the truck was carrying through the storm.

Then, out of nowhere, it hit me.

Not a thought.

Not a memory.

A sudden, wordless pulse: a crushing weight in my chest, a raw grief so ancient-feeling and immediate that it seemed to belong to something deeper than the hour I was in.

There was no reason for it. No tragedy in the rearview. No bad news on the radio. No conversation I had just replayed badly enough to explain it. Just the signal itself, loud and undeniable, reporting something the road did not contain.

A few weeks later, I was sitting in the middle of a different kind of storm: rush-hour traffic in downtown Atlanta. The air was thick with exhaust and the frustrated heat of a thousand idling engines. I was boxed in, thirty minutes behind schedule, and going nowhere.

Then it arrived again.

Not the weight this time.

Warmth.

Quiet, unearned warmth behind my ribs. A sudden, radiant joy as inexplicable as the grief had been.

In both moments, my head-brain immediately tried to capture the signal. Outside Laramie, it searched for a disaster to justify the ache. In Atlanta, it looked for a success to explain the light. It wanted a reason. A cause. A room it could build around what the body was reporting.

But the reason was not the point.

The weight and the warmth were the same kind of data. They were the body speaking before the story had found its sentence. The bio-loop's report arriving in the only language older than words: pressure, ache, expansion, warmth, contraction, heaviness, light.

We have located the self too often in the attic of the mind, among the rafters of narrative and the dust of logic. But when the signal is loud enough, the attic disappears. There is only the report: immediate, irreducible, certifying that something is alive enough to be touched by what is moving through it.

I felt.

And before any argument could be constructed about what the feeling meant, I was.

Like **I Am**, **I Feel** is a complete sentence with a particular pull.

It wants to complete itself.

Sit with it for a moment and see what happens.

You are feeling something right now.

Maybe you know what it is. Maybe you do not. Maybe it started small and grew loud before you had a name for it. Maybe something has been quiet so long you stopped noticing it was there. Either way — loud or quiet, named or unnamed — the body is signaling.

It does not stop because the mind has stopped listening.

I Feel is the turn toward that signal.

A curious shift in attention. The decision, however small, to stop moving away from what the body is saying and face it instead.

That shift is harder than it sounds. It requires an unoccupied moment, however brief. The story machine is already running explanations. The instinct is already reaching for action: fix it, analyze it, justify it, outrun it, dismiss it, wait for it to pass, make it stop.

I Feel asks for something different.

Turn here. Look at this.

Let the signal be present before deciding what it means or what must be done about it.

That is the whole bearing.

And the question that opens it is not *how?*

It is *what?*

How do I feel? can be answered too quickly. Fine. Okay. Tired. Stressed. Bad. Numb. The word may be accurate enough for conversation and still too thin for navigation.

What is here? asks for something closer. What is the body carrying? What is pressing? What is tight, warm, hollow, heavy, dim, sharp, alive?"

What has been running underneath the story?

What requires attending to?

How asks for a summary.

What asks for the signal.

That is where I Feel begins.

But the signal you turn toward may already be moving through a room the story has tuned. The body reports. The head-brain explains. The explanation changes the field in which the next report arrives. A tightening becomes evidence. Evidence becomes certainty. Certainty returns to the body as more pressure.

I Feel is not the fantasy of finding a pure signal untouched by meaning. It is the turn toward what is actually present in the body now — including the signal as it has been amplified, dimmed, narrowed, or colored by the story around it.

The signal is not the named emotion. Emotion with a name is a translation — and the translation happens later, and higher up, than most accounts suggest. The gut and heart have already been sending transmissions before the head-brain has had a chance to form an opinion about them. By the time the signal reaches conscious awareness, it is already carrying information. Already leaning toward or away, toward relief or alarm, toward contact or withdrawal.

What the head-brain adds is the label. The category. The narrative that organizes the felt sense into something recognizable. The constriction becomes anxiety. The weight becomes grief. The expansion becomes joy. These translations are useful — often necessary. But a translation is not the original.

What I Feel is asking you to reach is what the body was already saying before the head-brain found a word for it.

Not anxiety — the constriction anxiety is naming. Not grief — the specific weight grief describes. Not joy — the expansion joy points toward. The signal itself. Before the story. Before the label.

All that is needed is a pause, if one is available, long enough to allow what is present to be noticed.

Some channels may be easier to hear than others. Breath may be one of them. You do not have to change it. But you might simply feel it. The rhythm, the rate, where it lands in the body. Shallow and quick, held without realizing, slow and deep, uneven, paused, rushed. Breath is one part of the composition already playing.

Tension may be there, or it may be absent. Jaw, shoulders, gut, hands. The locked set of the face. The bracing you did not know you were doing. The places where the body has been holding a note so long it stopped sounding like a note and started sounding like normal.

Perhaps the quieter textures become audible. Weight. Tightness. Hollowness. Warmth. Pressure. Restlessness. A small ache in the chest or gut or throat that had not quite entered attention until you turned toward it. These are all tones in the same composition, channels in the same mix, parts of the body's report waiting to be heard together.

When I Feel seems compressed — when even feeling feels out of reach — breath and tension and physical sensation may still be audible. The nervous system cannot be commanded back into availability. But the body may still be reporting through small channels. Breath noticed without demand. Tension observed without judgment. Sensation allowed to be present without being forced into meaning.

You are not trying to fix the mix.

You are learning to hear what has been playing.

In your body. In the specific weight of it, in the place it lives when you are not thinking about it, in the way it announces itself without warning. A song. A smell. A particular quality of light that touches something you did not know was still tender. You may have been carrying it longer than you realize. Longer than you have had language for what it is.

What you find is signal. It may not be the whole truth about the world. It may not know why it is here. It may not know whether the danger is present or remembered, whether the ache belongs to this moment or to something older.

But it tells the truth of what the organism is carrying now — faithfully, without agenda, before the storyteller has revised the draft.

The signal is not evidence of failure.

It is evidence of life.

The bio-loop is doing what it has always done — registering, faithfully and without agenda, the truth of what it is to be this specific person, alive in this specific moment, carrying this specific weather.

Sometimes the signal is loud. Impossible to ignore. Demanding attention whether you are ready to give it or not.

Sometimes it dims.

The music that used to move something no longer reaches. The morning arrives without the small sense of aliveness that used to accompany waking. The storm has become a constant drizzle refusing to let any light in. The colors are slightly wrong. The textures muted. The whole of experience arrives through gauze.

The signal has not stopped. It has withdrawn into a range ordinary attention struggles to hear. Harder to reach, not because it is absent, but because the volume has fallen beneath the noise of everything else.

If this is where you are, the bearing still applies.

Perhaps more than ever.

The turn toward — even when what is found is dim, even when the signal is barely legible — is still a turn toward something real. The bio-loop has not stopped pointing. It is still faithful, even when it is quiet.

And sometimes the signal is not quiet at all.

Sometimes it is so loud that everything else has gone offline.

I once watched a boy on the children's unit where I was working stand perfectly still in the middle of a screaming room. He was not fighting, and he was not hiding. He was just there. If you looked at his face, the story was gone — no anger, no tears, only a flat gray distance. But if you stood near him, you could feel the frequency.

A fine, high-tension hum in his hands.

The locked set of his jaw.

A breath broken into shallow, jagged pieces.

He did not have a single word for it. His I Think had been blown out by the noise. But his I Feel was transmitting at full volume. In that moment, his body was giving the most honest report in the building. Not because he understood the storm. Not because he could explain it. Because his body was reporting it without disguise.

Dim or deafening, barely legible or overwhelming everything else, the signal is still the signal.

The bearing still applies.

You are not broken because the signal is hard to read. You may feel lost because something in you has been unheard, unnamed, or carried too long without answer.

And like any returning, the turn can become more familiar the more it is made. The signal may remain loud. The weather may remain weather. The turning can still become less frightening. Less like stopping helplessly in the middle of a storm, and more like remembering how to listen inside one.

Curiosity points inward.

That is the direction this bearing asks you to go.

— In Brief

You are feeling something right now.

Maybe it is clear. Maybe it is vague. Maybe it has been quiet so long you stopped noticing it was there. Either way, the body is signaling.

I Feel is a turn toward that signal.

Notice what is here before deciding what it means or what to do about it.

Ask *what is here*. Not *how do I feel*. What the body is carrying right now. Tightness. Weight. Warmth. Hollowness. Pressure. The signal before its name.

Let the signal be a signal before it becomes a named explanation.

Notice it honestly if you can.

Then let the right question be asked.

— Explored

Every living organism is continuously monitoring its own condition.

Homeostasis. Equilibrium. Stability. Balance. Viability. Sufficiency. Different words for the same basic requirement: the organism has to remain within a livable range. When something shifts outside that range, the body signals. It does not wait for language. It does not wait for interpretation. It reports.

At the biological level, feeling begins as valence: toward or away, ease or strain, enough or not enough, safe enough or too much. At the level of lived experience, **I Feel** is that signal becoming available enough to notice.

By the time a feeling reaches awareness, it has usually traveled far. The gut and heart have already contributed to the organism's report. The head-brain has already begun interpreting. The story may already be gathering around the signal, trying to name it, explain it, justify it, or move it toward action.

The gut does not manufacture what we feel in any simple or total way. It contributes to the neurochemical, inflammatory, metabolic, and interoceptive conditions the head-brain receives and interprets as mood, energy, vigilance, ease, or unease. The heart does not broadcast emotional truth like a secret oracle in the chest. Its rhythm participates in the organism's felt state and sends continuous information upward. The head-brain does not invent the whole experience from above. It receives, models, names, predicts, and explains what the body has already begun reporting.

This is why feeling is rarely clean by the time we notice it. The signal has already entered relationship with story.

The body reports. The head-brain explains. The explanation changes the field in which the next report arrives. A tightening becomes evidence. Evidence becomes certainty. Certainty returns to the body as more pressure. The signal and the story begin answering each other, each one shaping the conditions under which the next one appears.

This matters for I Feel.

The bearing is not asking for a pure signal untouched by meaning. That signal may no longer be available, if it ever was. I Feel turns toward what is actually present in the body now — the signal as it has been amplified, dimmed, narrowed, colored, or intensified by the story around it.

These signals do not all move at the same speed. Some arrive as sudden pulses: the drop in the stomach, the heat in the face, the sharp constriction before the story has caught up. Some build slowly: heaviness, flatness, fatigue, dread, the long ache that has been playing beneath the day. Some flood the field. Some fall so quiet they nearly disappear.

I Feel does not ask which kind of signal should count. It turns toward what is actually here.

What I Feel asks for is enough pause, when enough pause is available, for the signal to become more legible.

We cannot think our way to the signal. We can only let the named feeling stay present long enough to show what it is sitting on.

The Circuit is Live

Cogito ergo sum.

I think, therefore I am.

René Descartes, searching for the one thing that could not be doubted, found it in the act of thinking. If thinking is happening, something must be there to think. The thought became evidence of the thinker.

He found something real.

He did not find the earliest report.

Thinking can fail. The story machine can collapse into recursion. The narrator disappears into the narration. I Think, under sufficient load, may become unavailable as a usable bearing. Thought is extraordinary. It is irreplaceable. It gives memory sequence, gives experience language, gives us a way to model the world across time.

Thought is also fragile.

Antonio Damasio spent decades demonstrating what Descartes missed. His work with patients whose emotional processing had been impaired revealed something strange and important: reasoning can remain analytically active while decision becomes profoundly compromised. A person may compare options, list consequences, understand facts, and still be unable to arrive at lived decision. The body's feeling-tones are part of valuation. They help mark what matters.

Feeling is not noise interfering with reason.

Feeling is part of how reason finds weight.

Not philosophically. Biologically. I Feel is the current moving through the body — the spark of biological report made legible. It tells the organism that something matters, that something is pressing, that something is alive enough to be touched by what is moving through it.

I Am is the existential ground — the Compass's True North, the presence that persists beneath the storm, the one who holds the Compass. It is the orienting ground from which the bio-loop's signals can be received as signals rather than as identity. When I Am is lost, the Compass becomes unreadable — not because the signals stop arriving, but because there is no stable position from which to hold the instrument.

In a circuit, ground is not only foundation. It is the return path — the reference point a current requires to complete its movement. The spark needs somewhere to land. I Am is where it lands.

The signal is the biological spark. It is what the bio-loop cannot extinguish while the organism remains viable, because the signal is not an accessory to being alive. It is the body's evidence of aliveness. I Feel is the bearing that turns toward it.

Even when conscious feeling is dimmed, flattened, flooded, or hard to reach, the bio-loop is still reporting.

I felt, therefore I was does not replace Descartes' cogito. It corrects it at the level of embodiment. Descartes located certainty in thinking — the most fragile and conditionally available of the Compass bearings, the first to go under load. The body's correction is that aliveness is evidenced more basically by feeling: the current constantly running, the signal that persists when thinking cannot.

The Word We Reach For

We use the word *feel* for more than sensation. Notice this. Really notice it, because it points at something the bio-loop has always understood that the thinking mind has been slow to credit.

This situation doesn't feel right. You have said something like this. The grammar reaches for *feel* when what is being described is prior to analysis — a registered wrongness, a quality of mismatch, arriving before the argument for it has assembled.

Intuition is felt. The sense of danger that arrives before the reasoning about danger completes is felt in the body. The recognition of beauty, before any account of why it is beautiful, is felt. The experience of being genuinely known by another person — not evaluated, not assessed, truly known — is felt in a way that no description of it can replicate or replace.

Joy is felt.

Before it is an idea, before it is a goal, before it becomes something to pursue or explain, joy is a quality of aliveness in the body. Present or absent. Accessible or foreclosed.

Joy is not incidental to being alive. The capacity for it may be foundational to what we are — not a reward for sufficient achievement, not a byproduct of favorable conditions, but something we were built toward.

Wittgenstein observed that the limits of our language are the limits of our world. At the most ordinary level, the sentences we use shape what can be distinguished inside experience.

I am anxious does more than describe a state. It constructs one. It can place the weather into identity. It can hand I Am — the ground, the presence that persists beneath the storm — to the signal moving through it. It can collapse the distinction between the one experiencing the feeling and the feeling being experienced.

I feel anxious is not a gentler version of *I am anxious*. It is a structurally different claim. It keeps the ground where it belongs and the signal where it belongs — in the domain of I Feel, attended to by an I Am that has not been captured by it.

The small difference between those two constructions is not grammatical pedantry. It is the difference between being the storm and standing in it.

Our language reaches for *feel* across the whole range of embodied life: raw physical sensation, intuitive mismatch, grief, dread, beauty, recognition, longing, joy. That range is wide because we are always registering our relationship to what is. Pain and pleasure, contraction and expansion, toward and away, contact and withdrawal, dread and joy — all of them belong to the continuum of felt life.

That continuum is not incidental to being alive.

It is one of the ways life knows what matters.

The balance point between pleasure and pain — elusive, evasive, evocative, never quite captured, always slightly ahead — is the driver of everything the species has ever done to perpetuate itself. The bio-loop calibrated to seek the feeling that rewards the behaviors that propagate life. The ache of longing and the completion of its resolution. The specific way that reaching toward another person and being met produces a signal in us that nothing else quite replicates — because nothing else was designed to.

I Feel is the sentence closest to that current.

The signal that feels most private, most specifically yours, most evidence of the particular unrepeatable life you are living, is also the signal that connects you to every organism that has ever lived. The content is yours. The shape of the signal is ancient.

The body feels because it is alive.

And because it is alive, it keeps reporting.

When the Signal Floods or Fades

The signal can become hard to read in two directions.

The first is too much.

The signal overwhelms the other bearings, running so loud and so long without reception that it consumes the available field. The bio-loop escalates through every channel it can reach. The body becomes messenger. I Feel floods the room, and I Do begins gathering around urgency before the rest of the Compass can be held.

This is the direction most visible from the outside.

The person in acute distress.
The storm at full intensity.

The second direction is quieter. More insidious. Often more difficult to name.

The signal dims.

Anhedonia is the clinical word for part of this territory. But the word can feel too small for the reality it points toward. It is not only the absence of pleasure. It can feel like the fading of contact itself — the gradual or sudden dimming of the felt sense of being alive, present, touched by the world.

The music that used to move something in the body no longer reaches it. The food that used to be a sensory experience becomes fuel. The conversation that used to feel like genuine contact becomes an exchange of information between two systems that have forgotten how to touch. The morning arrives without the small sense of aliveness that used to accompany waking. Another day comes with the colors slightly wrong, the textures slightly muted, the whole of experience arriving through gauze.

This is suffering too.

Quieter than panic. Less visible than collapse. But suffering all the same.

The bio-loop does not stop when the felt signal dims. It keeps registering the organism's condition. It keeps reaching for viability. It keeps pressing toward some form of aliveness the organism can still feel.

That is where proxy becomes tempting.

A substance. A screen. A fantasy. A rush. A scroll. A purchase. A risk. A sensation strong enough to break through the gauze and confirm, for a moment, that something can still land.

The person reaching is not always trying to stop feeling. Sometimes they are trying to feel enough. Enough relief. Enough warmth. Enough intensity. Enough contact. Enough evidence that the current is still moving.

Addiction and compulsion often live here, where ordinary aliveness has become too dim, too painful, or too difficult to reach directly. The reach may be dangerous. The channel may become destructive. The consequences may be devastating. But the need underneath the reaching is not false.

The organism is trying to find the balance point.

We are reaching for something more basic than indulgence or escape: a felt state that is survivable. A place where the signal is present without becoming unbearable, where we can register ourself as alive without that registration becoming another source of suffering.

The logic is recognizable. The channel can still be costly.

A proxy can deliver real relief without answering the source. It can make the signal flare briefly and then leave the need still waiting. It can prove that feeling is possible while failing to restore contact, meaning, safety, nourishment, rest, grief, belonging, or whatever the original signal was trying to reach.

That is the trap.

The body receives something real. The deeper need remains unanswered. The signal returns. The person reaches again.

We are not broken. The bio-loop is faithful. The balance point it is reaching for is real. The problem is that the available channel cannot carry what the need requires.

The need is legitimate.

Relief is not the same as resolution.

What the Bio-Loop Cannot Know

The bio-loop cannot check the provenance of the signal it receives.

It reads the state of the organism and responds to that state as state. The felt sense of contact, aliveness, relief, intensity, warmth, stimulation, danger, or ease is real inside the body whether it came through physical presence, memory, imagination, screen, substance, story, relationship, or the chemical response produced by the organism's own neurological processes.

The bio-loop does not stand outside the signal and ask where it came from. It receives what arrives.

A screen can generate a real signal in the person. A remembered conversation can change the body. A fantasy can move chemistry. A substance can create relief the person feels as relief. A witnessed emotion can briefly feel like contact. The body receives something. The signal changes. The bio-loop responds honestly.

Then the signal fades.

And the need may still be there.

That is the problem with proxy. It delivers something. If it delivered nothing, it would be easy to abandon. It delivers something real enough for the body to receive. A flare of aliveness. A brief quieting. A sense of being reached. A moment of warmth, intensity, release, or contact.

The proxy succeeds just enough to be remembered.

Then it fails in the place that matters most.

The original need remains unanswered.

This is why the reach can repeat so quickly. We remember that something landed. The signal quieted, flared, moved, or changed. The next time the dimness returns, or the pain rises, or the loneliness presses, the old channel is easier to find.

The screen is not the whole problem. The substance is not the whole problem. The fantasy, the risk, the scroll, the purchase, the witnessed sensation — none of these is the whole problem by itself.

The need is older than the channel.

The channel becomes costly when it keeps delivering relief that cannot carry what the need requires. The body receives something real. The deeper need remains waiting. The signal returns. We reach again.

Proxy is not false relief. It is incomplete relief.

That is why it can become so difficult to leave behind.

When the Horizon Collapses

Under enough pain, dimness, urgency, exhaustion, shame, or accumulated unmet need, the field of possible futures can narrow until it no longer feels like a field.

We may stop encountering options as options. Continuation feels unbearable. The old channels no longer quiet the signal. The direct path to what is needed cannot be found from where the person is standing. The story machine may begin speaking in final terms. Always. Never. Nothing. No way. No one. Nowhere.

The horizon collapses.

From inside that collapse, the world can appear brutally simple. Keep enduring what cannot be endured. Escape what cannot be endured. Become what we cannot bear to become. Disappear from the field in which the demand is being made.

That narrowing is real as an experience.

It is not the whole truth.

The signal may be accurate. The pain may be real. The exhaustion may be real. The failure of every available proxy may be real. The fact that we cannot currently locate another path may also be real.

But the horizon seen from inside collapse is still a horizon seen from inside collapse.

It is a narrowed field, not the whole sky.

This is where the Compass has to stay humble. It is not a substitute for another person, a safe room, medical care, crisis support, or the kind of help that may be needed when the horizon has collapsed that far. Sometimes the bearing cannot be held alone. Sometimes I Am has to be borrowed from the steadiness of another human being until enough ground returns to hold it yourself.

Still, the Compass can name one thing honestly.

A collapsed horizon is not the same as an exhausted world.

The signal is still pointing. The need is still real. The available channels may have failed, but failed channels are not the same as the end of possibility.

The person has not run out of life.

They have run out of readable paths from where they are standing.

Those are not the same thing.

What the Bearing Asks

I Feel, as a Compass bearing, does not ask you to understand the signal. The bearing is not called I Understand. It does not ask you to analyze what you are carrying, trace it to its origin, assess its validity, or decide what it means about you.

It asks for something simpler and harder.

Turn toward the signal, when there is enough room to turn. Let it be present long enough to be recognized before it has to become explanation, verdict, proxy, or action.

The signal may not get quieter. The storm may not obey. The ache may not reveal its origin. The numbness may not lift because it has been noticed.

The relationship can still change.

A signal that has been running through every available channel may finally be received as signal. The body may no longer have to speak only through urgency, collapse, proxy, or pain. The weight may remain, but it is held differently when it is no longer mistaken for the whole self.

The felt sense, given room, may become more specific. It may begin to show what it has been carrying. A pressure may become grief. A restlessness may become loneliness. A craving may reveal contact. A numbness may reveal exhaustion. A flood may reveal a need that has gone too long without answer.

You are not alone in what you carry.

The specific weight is yours — unrepeatable, particular, belonging entirely to the life you are living. The fact of the weight is older than your life and larger than your story. It belongs to the structure of being alive in a body that signals, reaches, suffers, remembers, and keeps trying to find its way toward what it needs.

Every person who has lain awake at three in the morning with something they could not name.

Every person who has smiled at the right moments and felt nothing behind the smile.

Every person who has scrolled and scrolled looking for the thing that would finally land.

Every person who has reached for relief because the direct signal was too long unanswered to bear.

Every person who has carried the weight so long that the weight begins to feel like who they are.

That is not who you are.

That is what you have been carrying.

The Compass is in your hands.

The ground is beneath your feet.

The signal — your signal, the one that has been spinning faithfully through everything — is still pointing.

It has been pointing toward something real.

What is offered here is the working account of the signal — enough to turn toward it and read it. The deeper research on interoception, the clinical literature on felt sense and somatic awareness, and the fuller biological account of how the body generates and carries feeling will be available at
https://waynegwilliams.com/

CHAPTER 10 — I Need

What the bio-loop is actually requiring beneath the signal and story. Not the substitute or the proxy. The actual requirement. Let it show itself before naming it. Plainly, if you can.

One day while I was sitting with I Am, noticing thoughts and allowing them to complete, something appeared that I had never actually considered to be a thought. I had treated it as a true statement. It did not present as an option, or something to consider, or even as a desire. It arrived as fact.

I need to get high.

The sentence landed as requirement. As plain as thirst. As non-negotiable as hunger. My mind did not ask whether I wanted to. It did not say, this would feel good. It did not say, this is the road I know toward relief. It stated plainly what had to happen.

I need to.

That was the distortion. My body did not need to be high to remain alive. Something in me wanted relief. Something in me wanted the signal to change. Something in me knew an action that would alter the state quickly. But the sentence did not arrive as want. It arrived wearing the authority of need.

So I stayed with it and grew curious.

I went back to the stories before that sentence. They were not random. If the thought was about food, I needed nourishment. If the story was a recent conversation, the need was to be understood. If it had been about work, something in me needed security, competence, movement, or recognition. If it was a relationship story, something in me needed contact, belonging, repair, or the felt sense that I mattered to someone.

The false sentence had a true source.

That is what made it powerful.

The old route had lowered pressure before. It had changed the signal before. It had given me, in my body, something real enough to remember. So when the signal rose again, the route appeared quickly. The proxy spoke first — not as temptation, not as preference, but as requirement.

But I caught the thought as a story. That was I Think doing its job — recognizing the sentence not as a biological absolute, but as a narrative. A proxy. But catching the story didn't end the pull. Recognizing the story did not automatically turn off the body's response to it. It only cleared enough space to be curious of what was underneath.

What lived underneath was not another thought. It was a wanting so dense it had its own gravity. It was the physical pull toward the sensation itself — not the idea of it, not the memory of the ritual, but the body's blunt, heavy anticipation. The narrowing of the room. The hum in the nervous system preparing for the drop, the relief, the chemical exhale.

That was I Feel. The raw, unnarrated signal pulsing beneath the story.

I stayed with it. That was harder. Being curious helped.

The question I Need asks in that moment is not what do I feel? You already have that. The room is already thick with feeling. The question is: what is this feeling reaching toward? What does the proxy provide that feels so compelling, so vital to my viability, that the body is delivering it with the force of fact?

When I looked for the answer, I didn't find one. Not cleanly. The true requirement had been buried under years of the proxy doing the heavy lifting. The sensation of the high had become the object itself, paving over the original necessity so thoroughly that the root was opaque. Was it a starved hunger for belonging? An escape from the crushing weight of evaluation? Relief from a body that had forgotten how to settle without chemical help? I couldn't be certain. The exact label wouldn't surface.

What I found instead was the looking.

I didn't force an answer. I didn't demand that my biology explain itself. I just stayed near the ache of it. And the act of turning curiously toward the question provided something I hadn't expected.

The specific need never surfaced. But the behavior's claim to be a requirement began to loosen.

The proxy had been speaking through the voice of necessity. It claimed that if I did not obey it, I would not survive the moment. But the curiosity provided some clarity. By holding steady and asking, *what are you trying to solve?* the proxy was revealed as a reach toward resolution it could never actually provide.

That was enough.

The need did not magically resolve. But there was a loosening. The metallic grip on my chest released, not because the underlying need had been met but because the presentation had changed. The proxy loosened from requirement back into want. Oxygen returned to the room.

That is the bearing doing its job. Not fixing the storm. Changing enough to keep the Compass in hand.

That catching was only possible because I had created the conditions for it.

I was sitting with I Am. Deliberately curious. Giving my interior life a little time without an agenda — not managing it, not filling it, just allowing what was present to surface. That is not a natural posture in the modern world. It requires something the modern environment keeps distant: unoccupied time left unoccupied.

This is the irony.

We have not lost the capacity to notice what we need. We have lost the conditions that make noticing possible. Modernity can make it easier to meet our immediate needs. People can still find connection, meaning, and safety. But because there is always something more immediately engaging always within reach, it can make meeting deeper needs more complicated.

We are living in a miracle of efficiency, a world where the gap between a want and its fulfillment is collapsed to near zero. Hunger? An app brings a meal to your door in twenty minutes. Boredom? A billion hours of high-definition narrative live in your pocket. Isolation? A digital crowd is available at a tap and a thumb-swipe. Uncertainty? Three pages of explanation from a single prompt.

The purchase considered at breakfast is on the porch by evening. The conversation with the friend on the other continent is real-time, in her kitchen, while you sit in yours, sipping coffee, looking at her face on screen.

This is the crowning achievement of modernity: the elimination of the wait. This is astonishing. A human being in the twenty-first century has more of what they want, faster than any generation before could have imagined.

But there is a biological cost to this velocity. While our technology moves at the speed of light, the bio-loop still moves at the speed of life. Our wants now have fulfillment paths optimized for speed, while many of our needs have proxies that can imitate fulfillment before the need itself has had time to become legible.

The scroll, the feed, the notification now occupies the space of silence that was once available for connection-need to become audible. The bio-loop's signal requires a gap to surface into. We close the gap before the signal can speak.

The discomfort of unoccupied time has a message in it. We must be able to sit with the discomfort long enough for the message to surface.

I was intentionally being curious. That is how the thought surfaced. That is how I could catch it. The bearing I Need asks for those conditions long enough for the signal to become legible. To be more specific than noise.

The proxy's authority depends on the gap remaining closed.

The gap is where the need becomes audible.

That gap does not have to be large. It does not have to be peaceful, meditative, or clean. It may be only a breath, a few seconds of curiosity before the reach completes itself. The moment before the screen opens. Before the text is sent. Before the apology comes too quickly, the argument sharpens, the purchase is made, or the old route takes over with the familiar confidence of something that has worked before.

Inside that small space, the sentence can change.

I need this can become *something in me is reaching for this.*

That is not a small change.

The pressure may remain. The pull may remain. The old route may still glow with the authority it has earned through repetition. But the sentence has shifted. The proxy is no longer identical with the need. The reach has become visible as reach.

This is where I Need begins its actual work. It does not begin with a clean answer. It begins with a separation. The thing I am reaching for and the thing I require may not be the same.

They can be close. Food answers hunger. Sleep answers exhaustion. A difficult conversation may answer the need for repair. A door closing may answer the need for safety. A hand held in the right moment may answer the need for contact.

Sometimes they are only shaped alike.

Recognition can resemble belonging. Achievement can resemble meaning. Control can resemble safety. Stimulation can resemble aliveness. The resemblance is what makes the proxy convincing. It delivers something real enough for the body to register. Something lands. The signal changes. The route is remembered.

Then the unmet part remains.

That is why proxies can become so powerful. They are rarely nonsense. They usually solve something. They lower pressure. They interrupt pain. They provide sensation where there was numbness, quiet where there was noise, intensity where there was flatness, control where there was exposure, a feeling of contact where actual contact was too risky or too far away.

The question is not whether the proxy worked.

It did.

The question is what it worked for.

What pressure did it lower? What signal did it quiet? What did it give me, in my body, that I had not found another way to receive? What did it protect me from feeling, facing, risking, grieving, saying, needing?

These questions do not accuse the reach. They listen to it.

A drink may be carrying the shape of rest. A screen may be carrying relief from loneliness. An argument may be carrying the need to be heard. A performance may be carrying the need to matter. Withdrawal may be carrying the need for protection.

The behavior begins to reveal the need by the shape of what it keeps trying to solve.

This is why I Need can feel so strange at first. The bearing often starts with something that looks like the wrong direction. It begins with the craving, the irritation, the reach, the pressure, the old familiar move. The Compass does not turn away from those things too quickly. They may be the most legible evidence available. The need itself may still be hidden, but the route toward relief is visible.

So the bearing asks:

What was this reaching for?

That question has to be held carefully. Asked with accusation, it becomes another courtroom. Asked with urgency, it becomes another demand.

But when it is asked with curiosity and enough ground, it becomes a lantern.

It may reveal something ordinary first. Hunger. Thirst. Fatigue. Too much noise. Too many demands. The need to move the body. The need to stop answering. The need to be alone for a while. The need not to be alone anymore.

Ordinary needs become distorted when they are ignored long enough. A body that needs rest may speak in disgust. A body that needs food may speak in despair. A body that needs quiet may speak in rage. A body that needs help may speak in resentment. A body that needs contact may speak in criticism because criticism feels safer than reaching.

The signal is not lying.

The translation may be poor.

I Need is the bearing that stays close enough for the translation to improve.

The need may never surface clearly.

This is not a failure of the bearing. It is the bearing reporting honestly on the terrain.

Some needs were buried before they had names. Before the signal had language. Before the body had any way to know that what it was reaching for was a legitimate requirement rather than a weakness to be managed, hidden, or outrun. The proxy may have been in place so long it has become the landscape. The original need may be too far back, so entangled with early learning its direct expression is too dangerous to surface cleanly under attention alone.

Some terrain requires a guide, sometimes a trained one. That is still navigation. A Compass that points to another person is a Compass providing accurate direction.

The bearing I Need does not promise the need will become visible. But honest looking — patient, non-condemning, genuinely curious about what the reach has been trying to solve — is sufficient to begin changing the proxy's authority. Even if the need itself is not found, the proxy has been seen.

A proxy seen as a proxy is already less than it was.

It does not disappear. The pull may remain. The old route may still carry the weight of everything it has provided before. But it has lost the one thing its authority depends on: the certainty that this is what you need. That certainty is the grip.

The question shaped by curiosity is what loosens it enough to be noticed.

Once noticed, it has an address.

And what has an address can eventually be found.

— In Brief

Before the story. Before the feeling.

The need was there first.

It is the source of the signal. The reason the bio-loop keeps moving at all. And it is the hardest part to see.

The substitute doesn't close the gap.

I Need is the bearing that looks underneath for the actual requirement.

Sometimes it arrives plainly. I need rest. I need help. I need to be seen. I need to be safe. Plain. Simple. True.

You do not have to know yet how the need will be met. Notice it first. A need that has been noticed is different from a need that is still driving everything from underground.

A noticed need has an address. And what has an address can eventually be found.

— Explored

Underneath the story, there is something older.

It was there before the narrative began, before the story machine came online and started assembling explanations, predictions, and verdicts about who you are and what you can expect from the world. It was there before the signal you learned to turn toward in I Feel had been translated into anything the mind could name.

The need was there first. It is also the most consistently hidden thing in the bio-loop.

This seems paradoxical. The need is the engine — the source of the signal, the origin of the pressure, the thing whose unmet status sets the whole movement in motion. The loop registers requirement, sends signal, drives action. That spin keeps the organism on the living side of the line.

This is biology before it is metaphor. A bacterium has metabolic requirements. It detects chemical gradients. It moves toward what sustains it and away from what threatens it. The structure is ancient: requirement, signal, movement. In human beings, the pattern becomes vastly more complex, but the underlying movement remains.

The need is not a peripheral feature of our experience. It is the center of it. And yet it is the bearing that most consistently escapes notice.

In a simpler organism, the distance between requirement and movement is short. The need arises, the signal organizes response, and movement follows through the channels available to that form of life. The organism does not have to understand what it needs. It only has to answer the pressure.

In a human being, the distance is longer. Need still begins below language, but before it becomes available as I Need, it may pass through body state, affective signal, memory, prediction, relational history, shame, habit, culture, language, and the routes that have lowered pressure before. The underlying movement remains ancient: requirement, signal, movement. But the translation becomes crowded.

That is the paradox of this bearing. Need is first in the loop, but often late to awareness. By the time a person can say I need, the original requirement may already have been translated into urgency, story, proxy, demand, or the nearest available relief.

Need's signals are often loud. Hunger, loneliness, fear, shame, exhaustion, meaninglessness, longing — these do not whisper forever. They press. They intensify. They demand response. But the need itself rarely arrives cleanly. By the time the signal reaches consciousness, it has usually already been processed: filtered through memory, prediction, story, urgency, and available habit; translated into something nearer, faster, and easier to reach.

The body may be signaling for rest, and the mind hears escape. The body may be signaling for contact, and the mind hears control. The body may be signaling for meaning, and the mind hears achievement. The body may be signaling for safety, and the mind hears certainty.

That is the difficulty of I Need. The need is central, but it is often known indirectly — by the shape of the signal, by the substitute that promises relief, by the story that forms too quickly around it, by the ache that remains after the proxy has done its temporary work. We do not usually begin by seeing the need directly. We begin with what has become available: the signal, the story, the reach, the substitute, the field around the missing thing.

That is where the bearing begins.

What Counts as Need

A need is not simply something wanted with intensity. Intensity can belong to need, but intensity alone does not prove the source. A want may be vivid. A craving may be urgent. A demand may feel non-negotiable. None of those qualities, by themselves, tell us whether the bio-loop is pointing at an actual requirement or at the nearest available relief.

A need is a requirement for viability.

That word has to be held broadly enough to fit a human life. Food, water, sleep, warmth, movement, safety, and physical contact are needs because the body cannot remain well without them. But human viability is more than cellular survival. A human being also requires connection, self-authorship, meaningful engagement, competence, belonging, truth, rest, repair, and the felt sense that life is occurring inside conditions that can be lived in.

These are not luxuries added after survival. They belong to the kind of organism we are.

Other needs are harder because their routes are less direct. The need for connection may arrive as irritation. The need for rest may arrive as disgust. The need for repair may arrive as an argument that keeps rehearsing itself. The need for meaning may arrive as flatness. The need for safety may arrive as control. The need for grief may arrive as numbness.

The signal is real.

The translation may be wrong.

A want is different. A want is the object or experience the system reaches toward. Wants are not bad. They are often beautiful. Desire gives life texture, direction, color, appetite, play, imagination, longing. A want may carry a true need very closely. I want food may be the body's direct route to nourishment. I want to call my friend may be connection becoming legible. I want to quit this job may be the first honest sentence after a long season of collapse.

Wants become difficult when they are mistaken for proof. I want this, therefore I need this. I want this intensely, therefore this must be the requirement. I cannot stop thinking about this, therefore this must be what the signal is asking for.

Sometimes that is true.

Often enough, it is incomplete.

A proxy lives in that incompleteness. A proxy is a route that changes the signal without meeting the source. It borrows the authority of need and the accessibility of want at the same time. It presents with the urgency and conviction of genuine requirement — *I need this, I cannot survive this moment without it* — while actually delivering the partial relief of a want addressed through an adjacent channel.

The proxy is not random. It is almost always pointing in the right direction. The person reaching for the drink is reaching toward something real — rest, relief, connection, the quieting of a signal that has been running too long. The proxy borrows the shape of what is actually needed and delivers something close enough for the bio-loop to register as landing.

That landing is what makes the proxy so difficult to see through. They are not imaginary. They work at one level. The alcohol warms. The scroll distracts. The purchase creates movement. The argument releases pressure. The achievement lands. The fantasy gives the body a shape of contact. The plan gives uncertainty something to hold. The apology lowers threat. The withdrawal protects the exposed vulnerability.

Something changes.

The question is whether the need was met.

If the proxy delivered nothing, it would be easy to abandon. It delivers something. Something real enough for the body to remember. The route is reinforced. The next time the signal rises, the proxy appears quickly — not as temptation, not as preference, but with the full conviction of requirement. The false sentence arrives wearing the authority of a fact.

The easiest way to distinguish between them is by asking what happened after it. Did the signal resolve, or only change form? Did the body settle, or did it require the same route again soon after? Did the action nourish the life around it, or did it narrow the life around it? Did it bring the system closer to contact, rest, truth, safety, repair, and ok-ness — or did it purchase a short quiet at the cost of more distance from those things?

These questions help distinguish the three:

A need is the requirement underneath the signal.

A want is the thing I consciously desire or reach toward.

A proxy is the want or action that quiets the signal while failing to meet the requirement.

In lived experience, they overlap. A want can be need-aligned. A proxy can contain a real piece of what the need requires. A need can be so buried that only the proxy is visible. This is why I Need requires patience.

There is a layer beneath the needs themselves.

Edward Deci and Richard Ryan, across four decades of research, identified three psychological needs that appear universally present across cultures, developmental stages, and the full range of human circumstance. The needs they identified, and are most often studied in human psychology, are autonomy, competence, and relatedness. The names are useful if we keep them close to life.

Autonomy is the need for authorship — the felt sense that my action belongs to me, that I am not merely being pushed, coerced, managed, or carried by forces I cannot own.

Competence is the need for effective engagement — the felt sense that my actions can meet the world, that effort can become movement, that difficulty can be encountered without becoming immediate defeat.

Relatedness is the need for received connection — the felt sense that I matter to someone, that I am known by someone, that my presence registers in another human being without having to be performed into existence.

When these needs are available, a person does not merely feel happier. The system has more room. Action feels more authored. Challenge feels more workable. Relationship feels more receivable. The bio-loop has better conditions to answer what is required.

When these needs are blocked, the signal does not politely stay in its category.

A blocked need for autonomy may appear as control. If I cannot feel authorship, I may try to manage every variable.

A blocked need for competence may appear as achievement or avoidance. If I cannot feel effective, I may chase measurable proof, or refuse the arena where failure could be seen.

A blocked need for relatedness may appear as attention, validation, performance, or careful proximity. If I cannot receive connection safely, I may reach for signs that resemble connection without requiring the full vulnerability of being known.

These substitutes make sense. Control resembles autonomy because both change the field of action. Achievement resembles competence because both deliver evidence of effectiveness. Attention resembles relatedness because both involve being registered by another. The resemblance is the hook. It lets the body receive something close enough to remember.

Then the unmet part remains.

Beneath all of this is safety.

Before we can reach toward autonomy, competence, or relatedness, we have to answer a more ancient question: *am I safe enough to continue?*

Safe, here, does not mean comfortable, certain, or free from difficulty. It means safe enough that the person is not organizing themself entirely around emergency. Safe enough that the threat-response architecture is not redirecting every available resource toward survival, leaving nothing for the slower, more deliberate work of noticing what is actually needed.

That prior condition is not a fourth need sitting beside the others. It is the substrate the others require in order to become accessible at all.

Consider what happens to each need when that substrate is absent.

Autonomy requires enough safety for action to feel self-authored. Under threat, we do not experience ourselves as the source of our movement. We experience ourselves as responding — the ancient architecture executing, the signal driving, the action happening before deliberation has had time to engage. The need for autonomy is still present. The condition that makes self-authorship feelable is not.

Competence requires enough safety because learning and effectiveness need room. A system in emergency does not naturally expand into challenge. It narrows. It reaches for speed, certainty, familiar action, and the path most likely to reduce immediate danger.

Relatedness requires this condition most directly. What addresses the relatedness need is not proximity or social contact or the performance of connection. It is the experience of being genuinely received by another person — and that experience requires vulnerability. Vulnerability requires us to have assessed the relational environment as safe enough to risk exposure. The person whose nervous system learned, at significant cost, that closeness produces harm may be unable to receive genuine connection even when it is available and offered sincerely. The need is present and pressing. The safety condition required to approach it has not yet been established.

So the body reaches for what can be approached without that exposure.

Control instead of safety. Achievement instead of meaning. Attention instead of contact. Certainty instead of ground. Numbing instead of rest. Stimulation instead of aliveness. Proximity instead of reception.

The proxy appears where the direct route feels unavailable.

The signal keeps running because the proxy cannot close the gap the need is pointing toward. And the gap cannot be closed because the prior condition that would make the legitimate channel accessible is not yet present.

I Need is the bearing that follows the imitation back toward the requirement.

What does this actually require?

Not merely what would quiet it.

What would answer it?

When Safety Was Not Learned

Safe enough is learned before it is understood.

The infant does not arrive able to name hunger, fear, loneliness, overstimulation, or the need for contact. It arrives able to signal. The cry, the reach, the gaze, the turning away, the body tightening or settling — these are broadcasts before they are reports. Something is required, and the body sends the signal before the child can know what the signal means.

What happens next teaches the body how need works.

When that signal is received accurately enough, often enough, the body begins learning a basic grammar: this feeling points somewhere; this pressure can be answered; this need can be brought into relationship without making the world more dangerous.

When the signal is received accurately enough, the infant learns the foundational lesson of the bio-loop: my internal states have an outside address. What I carry can be brought into the world. The pressure that rises in me can be answered by something beyond me. That learning is not cognitive. It arrives before language, before reflection, before the child can form any explicit understanding of what is happening. It is written into the body's calibration of what signals are for and what the world can be expected to do with them.

This is the foundation interoceptive legibility is built on. Not a skill developed in isolation, but a capacity that emerges from the relational environment consistently demonstrating: your signal means something. What you are carrying can be received. The need underneath the broadcast has an answer, and bringing it into relationship does not make the world more dangerous.

When that foundation is established, the bearing I Need has ground to work from. The adult who learned this early can follow a signal toward its source with some confidence that what they find there is real, nameable, and potentially addressable. The need may still be obscured by story, urgency, or proxy. But the basic trust that the signal points somewhere worth following is present.

When the signal is not received — when it is consistently missed, misread, met with withdrawal, met with alarm, met with something that increases the pressure rather than answering it — a different grammar forms.

Not: my needs are unmet.

But: my signals are not safe to send.

That is the distinction that matters. The child does not conclude that the need is illegitimate. The child concludes that expressing the need is dangerous. The signal gets rerouted. Not because the bio-loop stopped generating it — the loop is faithful, always — but because the organism learned, at significant cost and under conditions that made the lesson reasonable, that surfacing the signal produced outcomes worse than bearing it alone.

The need went underground.

The architecture built to keep it there was not pathology. It was intelligence. The child who learned not to signal, not to reach, not to show the pressure — that child was doing the most adaptive thing available under the conditions present. The bio-loop kept spinning. The child kept surviving. The route that was chosen, sometimes by default, kept the signal from making survival harder.

The proxy may feel like the need because it is the route the need has been using for years.

The adult who reaches for control may not be refusing trust. They may be carrying a body that learned safety only through management. The adult who cannot ask for comfort may not be proud or cold. They may be carrying a body that learned comfort was dangerous to need. The adult who performs competence past exhaustion may not be chasing vanity. They may be carrying a body that learned mattering had to be produced.

This does not make every route harmless. Some routes begin as protection and become costly. Some preserve life while narrowing it. Some reduce immediate danger while making real contact harder to receive. The point is not to excuse the route. It is to understand why the route has authority.

I Need has to move with care here.

A need that was hidden for survival cannot always be summoned by attention. The body may protect it by refusing to name it. It may offer only the proxy, the defense, the numbness, the ache around the place where language should be. That does not mean the bearing has failed. It means the bearing has found the protection around the need.

The protection is information too.

A wall tells us where something was not safe to expose. A blankness tells us where language may never have developed. A repeated proxy tells us which route the system trusted when the direct route was unavailable.

Sometimes this is as far as the Compass can go alone.

Some terrain requires another person — not because the Compass has failed, but because the original injury happened in the field where signals were supposed to be received. A need that became hidden in relationship may need relationship to become legible again. A therapist, a sponsor, a trusted friend, a partner, a group, a steady witness: someone who can help hold the field without forcing the need to appear before the body is ready.

That is still navigation.

The Compass that points toward another person is not pointing away from the work. It may be pointing toward the condition the work requires.

When Relief Becomes the Road

The proxy has to be understood before its cost can be seen clearly.

The bio-loop reaches for what has worked before. The route that lowered pressure once becomes the route most readily found when pressure rises again. That is not stupidity. It is the system doing what systems do — reinforcing what produced relief.

The Compass asks one more question: *worked for what?*

A route that lowers pressure is doing something real. The drink, the screen, the argument, the purchase, the fantasy, the achievement, the withdrawal, the apology offered too quickly — each one may be answering a signal the person has not yet been able to name.

The route may be costly. It may be incomplete. It may leave the actual need untouched. But it became available because something in the system was trying to survive the moment.

This is where the question matters.

Gabor Maté, working for years with people whose addictions had become devastatingly costly, asked a question that changes the whole room:

Why the pain?

That question does not romanticize the behavior. It does not erase consequence. It does not pretend the harm is harmless. It simply refuses to treat the reach as the deepest fact. It turns toward the pain the reach has been trying to answer.

What is this solving?

What signal did it quiet?

What need could not find another road?

Those questions reach toward I Need. The behavior may be dangerous, destructive, narrowing, or unsustainable. Still, underneath it, something has been asking for relief. The proxy may have provided warmth, distance, numbness, intensity, contact, quiet, control, or a momentary sense that the system could keep going.

That answer can carry terrible cost.

The tragedy is that the thing that works at the level of immediate relief can destroy the life it is trying to protect. It can quiet the signal while leaving the need untouched. It can keep the person moving while consuming the conditions that would have made another route possible.

The proxy is meaningful because it worked somewhere.

It is dangerous because the place where it worked was not the same place the need was waiting.

The question *why the pain?* reaches toward the need. The question *what is wrong with you?* buries it further.

That is why the Compass begins with curiosity here. The old road is not evidence that the person is stupid, weak, ruined, or hopeless. It is evidence that something has been trying to answer pressure with whatever road could be found.

The first task is to understand what that road has been carrying.

From there, its cost can finally be seen honestly.

The proxy that worked yesterday may work less well today.

In addiction literature, this is called tolerance: the same dose producing a diminishing effect, requiring more to achieve the same relief. But the pattern is not limited to substances. The scroll that used to soothe requires more scrolling. The control that once made the room feel safe has to reach farther, manage more, tighten more of the field.

What once registered as relief becomes baseline.

The signal returns. Sometimes at the same volume. Sometimes louder, because the proxy has introduced its own costs into the system. The gap has not closed. The available tool is losing its edge. So the body reaches again, with more urgency, through the road it already knows.

This is how proxy becomes compulsion.

The person is not simply failing to apply enough willpower. The bio-loop is operating faithfully: registering unmet need, driving toward relief, reinforcing the pathway that produced relief before. Escalation is faithfulness expressed through a channel that cannot reach the source.

That is why the old route can become so hard to leave. It is still carrying evidence. It still remembers the first relief, the first quiet, the first time the pressure dropped enough to breathe. Even after the cost becomes obvious, the body may keep reaching for the road that once proved it could change the signal.

The tragedy is not that the proxy does nothing.

The tragedy is that it does less and asks more.

As the proxy keeps failing to address the underlying need, the range of available responses contracts.

The road that was once one option among several becomes easier to find than anything else. Part of this is repetition. Pathways used often become more available. The body learns the turn. The reach becomes familiar. The sequence shortens: signal, pressure, road.

Part of it is consequence.

Relationships strain. Work becomes unstable. Health deteriorates. Money disappears. Trust thins. Time is consumed by the proxy and its repair.

The resources that might have supported a different kind of reaching are consumed by the proxy and its consequences.

This is how a channel narrows. What began as one available path can become, through repetition and cost, the only path the body can still clearly see. The person is no longer standing before a full table of options and casually choosing the worst one. They are moving inside a field the old road has been shaping for a long time.

This is why willpower-only answers fail.

They ask the person to choose differently while leaving untouched the conditions that make different choices accessible. The bio-loop is still signaling. The need is still unmet. The most available channel is still the proxy. Demanding that the person simply stop reaching asks the bio-loop to stop doing what it does.

The better question is not only how do we stop the proxy?

It is how do we make another channel reachable enough for the body to survive choosing it?

Punishment moves in the wrong direction.

It can interrupt behavior. It can raise the cost. It can frighten, contain, separate, or force temporary compliance. Sometimes containment is necessary. Harm has to be stopped. Consequences still matter.

But punishment cannot resolve the need the proxy has been answering.

Shame adds threat to a system already struggling to find a livable route. The body that has been reaching through the only channel it can clearly see now has more danger to manage, more exposure to survive, more reason to hide, defend, collapse, or reach again for the thing that has lowered pressure before.

Threat narrows the field.

That is the opposite of what I Need requires.

The bio-loop cannot be punished into legibility. It cannot be shamed into deeper understanding. It cannot be frightened into honest translation. Shame may produce concealment.

Punishment may produce compliance. Fear may interrupt the reach for a while. None of these teaches the body what the signal was pointing toward.

Navigation asks better questions.

What pressure did this lower?
What signal did this quiet?
What need was trying to survive through this route?
What would make another channel reachable enough to choose?

Those questions do not excuse harm. They make repair more possible because they move toward the source instead of merely striking the symptom. A person can take responsibility for the damage a proxy caused while also learning why the proxy had so much authority. The two belong together. Accountability without legibility becomes punishment. Legibility without accountability becomes evasion.

The Compass is trying to hold both.

The old road has to be seen clearly: what it carried, what it cost, what it protected, what it damaged, and what it could never finally provide. Then the question can move from accusation to direction.

What would answer the need more honestly?

That is the beginning of another channel. Not the full road yet. Not the action yet. That comes with I Will / I Do. Here, the work is to locate the need closely enough so that the next road can begin to appear.

A proxy seen clearly is already less absolute than it was.

A need named honestly is no longer buried in the dark.

And a channel that can be seen as a channel is no longer the whole world.

What the Compass Can Find

After all of this, the bearing I Need may sound as if it should produce one clean answer.

Sometimes it does.

The signal settles enough for the requirement beneath it to become plain. Rest. Food. Water. Sleep. Movement. Contact. Quiet. Safety. Repair. Grief. Truth. The ending of something that has gone on too long. The beginning of something that has been postponed so long it has become ache.

Those moments have their own mercy. The fog thins. The body's report becomes more specific. The reach finds its source. The person can say, with some clarity, this is what I need.

Often, the Compass finds something less direct first.

It may find the proxy. The old road. The route that lowered pressure, changed the signal, and carried the authority of need because it was the only reachable answer for a long time.

It may find the wall. The place where language stops. The blankness around the need. The defense that rises before the sentence can form. The tightening, numbing, explaining, pleasing, leaving, managing, or collapsing that appears whenever the direct route comes too close.

It may find the cost. The life narrowed around the channel. The relationships thinned. The trust spent. The body tired from reaching the same way and receiving less each time.

It may find another person.

That is still navigation.

The Compass is not failing when it points toward help. It is telling the truth about the terrain. Some needs became hidden in relationship and may become legible again only in relationship.

Some signals need a steady witness before they can become words. Some routes require someone trained, patient, and safe enough to help hold the field while the body learns that the old danger is not the only possible answer.

A reading does not have to be complete to be useful. The need may remain partially hidden. The proxy may remain strong. The wall may still stand. The old road may still be the easiest road to find.

But something has changed when the terrain has been named.

A proxy seen clearly is less absolute than it was.

A wall recognized as protection is no longer only obstruction.

A blankness understood as information is no longer empty.

A need located even roughly is no longer driving everything from underground.

That is what I Need gives back first: not a finished road, but coordinates. The signal has a direction. The reach has a history. The proxy has a purpose. The wall has a reason. The absence has a shape. The body is not merely making noise. It is reporting.

Once the report has been heard, even imperfectly, the Compass begins to turn.

The question changes from *what is happening in me?* to *what will I do with what has been found?*

That question belongs to the next bearing.

I Will / I Do does not begin with perfect certainty. It begins with the need as clearly as it can be read from here. It asks what movement can honor that reading without handing the whole field back to the old road.

Sometimes the movement is small. Eat. Sleep. Step outside. Ask for help. Make the call. Let the grief have ten honest minutes. Let another person know where you are.

Sometimes the movement is larger. End the pattern. Seek treatment. Change the conditions. Repair what can be repaired. Build another channel slowly enough that the body can survive choosing it.

The next bearing will not ask for a performance of strength. It will ask for movement that follows the reading.

The Compass can point.

And once it points, the next question can finally be asked:

What now?

The account of need presented here is compressed. The full attachment literature, the developmental research on how needs become invisible, the clinical work on substitution and its costs, and the broader empirical warrant for what the bio-loop actually requires will be available at
https://waynegwilliams.com/

CHAPTER 11 — I Will / I Do

I Will / I Do — The only bearing anyone else can see. I Will — intention present. I Do — bio-loop executing. The gap between them is not failure. It is information.

This is the only bearing the world sees.

Everything else in the bio-loop — the need pressing, the signal spinning, the story assembling, the ground holding or giving way — happens in the interior. Inaccessible to anyone watching from the outside. The only thing visible is the action. What you say. What you do. How you move through your life and your relationships.

The world reads this bearing and draws conclusions about who you are and what you can be expected to do next.

Those conclusions are almost always reading the output and calling it the person. They are not the same thing.

A man is pulled over on a dark road. His hands are shaking on the wheel. His answers come out clipped, defensive, then suddenly louder than the situation calls for. The officer reads confrontation and escalates. The man was already under load the officer never saw — a job lost that week, a son in the hospital, a nervous system that had learned long ago that flashing lights in the rearview mean something worse is about to happen. The behavior the officer is reading as attitude is the bio-loop executing with the narrowest possible gap between signal and action. The officer's escalation feeds back into the loop as new threat. The loop produces more of what the officer is reading as attitude. By the time the encounter ends, the driver is in custody, charged with obstruction and resisting, and the story written in the police report describes a character. The character is the bio-loop's output under load the report never mentions.

A twelve-year-old girl is removed from her home. Two weeks later she is separated from the younger brother she has been parenting since she was seven, because no single placement could take them both. She stops eating. She refuses to speak to her caseworker. She is "disrespectful" and destroys property in the foster home. A diagnosis is written: oppositional defiance disorder. The diagnosis describes her behavior accurately. It describes nothing about what her bio-loop is actually signaling. The only ground under her feet has given way, the only stability she has ever known has been taken from her, and the system reading her behavior and controlling her circumstances assigns the label as character because it has no access to where that loss is processed and held.

A man six months sober walks into his brother's wedding. The open bar is the first thing he sees. His sister-in-law hands him a glass of champagne for the toast before he can say no. He excuses himself, finds a quiet hallway, paces, texts his sponsor, returns to the reception looking distracted and does not make the toast. His family reads him as ungrateful. As selfish. As making the day about himself. What the family is reading as character is the bio-loop doing the most sophisticated work it has done in six months — recognizing a threat the rest of the room could not see, routing around it, staying sober. From the outside, the visible node looks like failure. From inside, it is the closest thing to I Will the man has produced all year.

Three people. Three rooms. Three readings that are confident and wrong.

There is a spectrum here.

At one end is I Will — intention flowing into action. The ground present enough, the signal legible enough, a breath-sized gap between impulse and movement in which something that could be called choosing becomes possible. The person home when the action happens.

That gap is held open by what this book will call Deliberate Presence — the capacity for slow, considered, intentional response that makes the bearing readable. A finite resource. It depletes through use. It fatigues under load. The conditions that deplete it most are the exact conditions under which it is most needed.

At the other end is I Do — the bio-loop executing without that gap. The person is still present to their own loop. But Deliberate Presence has compressed below the threshold where the gap can stand. The action is still theirs, generated by their need, their signal, their body moving through their life. What is temporarily unavailable is the gap in which they could be present to it before it happens.

Most of life is lived between those two ends. The intention present but the signal loud. The ground there but compressed. The gap narrow. The next available thing presenting itself.

The next available thing.

This is the most honest description of how most behavior happens most of the time. Not the action a person would choose from full clarity and stable ground. The action most accessible given the conditions present when the bio-loop required movement. Action related to the intention. Reaching toward the right thing. But arriving through a proxy — not of need this time, but of will. The person genuinely trying to act from I Will and landing somewhere adjacent, because the Compass was readable but not steady.

You meant to speak calmly. You spoke calmly, but with an edge you didn't intend. The words were the right words. The tone told a different story. You heard it leave your mouth before you could recall it.

You meant to listen. You listened, and halfway through what she was saying you were already composing your response. You were present. You were not entirely there. The listening happened. So did the rehearsal underneath it.

You meant to stop at one. You stopped at two. Not because you decided differently. Because the first one didn't quite arrive, and the second one was already in your hand before the gap between them had opened wide enough for the question to be asked.

This is not failure. This is the bio-loop navigating with what it has.

The distance between I Will and I Do is not a moral distance. It is a load distance. When the load is lighter — needs are addressed, signal quieter, ground less compressed — the gap widens. When the load is heavier, the gap narrows. Sometimes to nothing. The person acts because the loop presses. The behavior is enacted because the signal required a response and the next available thing is whatever was within reach.

What the Compass makes possible over time is a wider gap. More breath. More space between the signal and the action in which the person can be present to what is happening before it happens. Not through repetition of the Five Sentences — through what the sentences make visible. Need addressed closer to its source. Accumulated signal reduced. The ground incrementally less compressed.

Not control. Presence.

The person home when the action happens.

Where this matters most is in the places it took longest to become legible. Not the single moment under load. The accumulated weight of a thousand next-available-things, arriving through the only visible node, read as character by the person watching — and eventually by the person doing the acting. The verdict written while the loop was still signaling. The character installed over the person who was always only a bio-loop pressing toward what it required.

I want to tell you about my ex-wife.

Not to assign blame — we both have our own account of what happened between us, and hers is as true from where she was standing as mine is from where I was standing, which is to say that both of us were inside a system neither of us had instruments to read. I want to tell you about her because this is where the Compass first showed me something about me I could not have seen without it. Something I needed to see. Something that arrived, when it arrived, with the specific weight of understanding that comes too late to change what happened but not too late to change what it means.

During the years of our marriage, and more acutely in the years of its dissolution, her behavior was — from where I stood — at times, inexplicable. There were patterns I could not account for. Actions that seemed designed to cause harm. Responses disproportionate to what had happened. A persistence in certain behaviors that, from the outside, read as vindictiveness. As intentional. As choices she made, repeatedly, about who she wanted to be in relation to me and to the life we had built and were in the process of dismantling.

My behavior was, of course, completely reasonable. My choices at the time seemed completely rational, justified, and understandable, given the circumstances.

I attributed her choices to character. That is what the visible node produces — the impression of character, of intention, of a person choosing to be the way they are.

What I can now see clearly is that her perspective was the same as mine. From where she stood my behavior was inexplicable, seemed designed to cause harm. Vindictive. Intentional. She could not understand why I could not see her. Why I could not just give her what she needed. Why I couldn't just be the person she needed me to be.

I was wrong. So was she. Not about the behavior — the behavior was real, its effects were real, the damage it produced was real. But neither of us could see what was driving it.

What I understand now, looking through the bio-loop that I couldn't see then, is this:

We were carrying needs that were not being met. Had not been met, in some cases, for longer than our marriage had existed — needs that preceded us, that our bio-loops had been spinning since long before we met, that had developed elaborate and sophisticated structures to manage and substitute for and route around the actual needs we had, because somewhere early and at significant cost, the direct expression of those needs had not been safe.

The need for safety. And the felt sense that the ground was not going to move. That what each of us had could not arbitrarily be taken. She needed to know that her existence was not contingent on the continued goodwill of someone who could withdraw it. I withdrew it. I needed to know my vulnerability, once exposed, would be received and reciprocated. She couldn't.

She did not need to be evaluated or assessed or managed or accommodated. She needed to be seen. Truly seen. The felt experience of being known by another person — the signal the bio-loop generates when genuine contact is made — one of the most fundamental requirements the human organism carries. I was too focused on my needs to meet hers.

I needed to be accepted as I was, not managed, evaluated, or assessed. I needed to be held. Truly held. The felt experience of being a part of another person — the signal the bio-loop generates when genuine acceptance is offered, unconditionally — another of the fundamental requirements the human organism carries. She had needs that had to be met before she could meet mine. I didn't meet them. I didn't know how.

We both needed our own version of belonging that did not require performance. The exhausting work of maintaining the version of ourself that was acceptable, legible, safe to present — and underneath it, the need to simply be seen and held, without the performance, in a space where we could hold and see each other. We tried. We ultimately felt we didn't belong with each other.

These were real needs. They were generating real signals. The signals were driving real actions — the behavior we were reading as vindictiveness, as intentional harm, as a character choosing to be difficult. None of it was chosen in the way I understood choosing. It was the bio-loop doing exactly what the bio-loop does. Pressing toward what was required. Using whatever channel was available. Expressing outward, through the only visible node, the next available thing. The full accumulated pressure of needs that had been present without adequate address for a very long time.

I did not see the needs. I was inside my own loop, with my own unread signals, constructing my own stories about what was happening and what it meant. So was she. We had both made conclusions from the stories we were telling ourselves about the type of person the other was. And from that conclusion, the verdict was pronounced.

I did not have the understanding, the instrument. I had not developed the capacity to see beyond the behavior. To look past the chosen actions and locate the needs under the expressed feelings. Neither did she. Neither of us had ever been handed a Compass.

What I feel now, sitting with this, is not absolution. What happened, happened. The damage was real. The grief of the dissolution was real, and it belonged to both of us.

What I feel is compassion. The specific, clarifying compassion that arrives when you finally understand better what someone was carrying underneath what they were doing. The way the behavior that looked like an irrational choice made sense once the need underneath it is considered long enough to be made visible.

We were not trying to cause harm. We were trying to survive and address the needs our bio-loop was signaling had to be met. With no Compass. In a storm that had been unnavigated for a very long time — pressing toward what was required through whatever channel remained open.

A person sees behavior, attributes it to character. A person holding the Compass can learn to see behavior as needs expressed. These are not the same thing and they do not produce the same response.

The world's response to visible behavior — judgment, consequences, rejection — feeds back into the bio-loop as new signal. As threat. As confirmation of whatever story is already running about who this person is and what they can expect. The bio-loop receives the response, processes it through the same system that generated the behavior in the first place, and produces more of the same. The response to the output becomes input. If the input is threat, the bio-loop generates more threat response.

This is not a mystery. It is the bio-loop doing what bio-loops do.

What changes — slowly, incrementally, with continued patience rather than perfection — is the returning. The signal recognized sooner. The story seen sooner. The need surfacing more directly. The action landing a little closer to what was actually intended.

Enough that the gap between I Will and I Do begins to widen. Enough that, more often, what you will is what you do.

And when you look at someone else — at the behavior the world is reading as character — you can see it too. The bio-loop expressing what was within reach. The next available thing. The same structure running in every bio-loop that has ever pressed toward what it required.

Not character. Load.

The recognition of that difference changes what becomes possible between people.

— In Brief

This is the bearing the world sees.

Everything else — story, feeling, need — happens inside. What becomes visible is action. What you say. What you do. How you move.

I Will is intention present. The gap between impulse and movement open enough for choosing to stand there.

I Do is the bio-loop executing. Action without that gap. Not absence. Compression.

Most of life is lived between those ends. The distance is not moral. It is load.

The gap can widen. Needs addressed closer to the source. Signal quieter. Ground less compressed. More breath between the signal and the action.

Not control. Presence. The person home when the action happens.

— Explored

The spectrum between I Will and I Do — intention flowing into action at one end, the bio-loop executing without deliberation at the other — is where every human behavior lives. What varies is where on that spectrum any given action originates. And from the outside, there is no way to know.

This is the structural limitation that shapes most everything human beings have ever built to assess, manage, and respond to each other.

What Observation Cannot Reach

The entire apparatus of social judgment is built on the visible node. Reputation. Consequence. Reward and punishment. The legal system's assessment of culpability. The psychiatric system's diagnostic categories. The relational world's ongoing evaluation of who a person is and whether they can be trusted and what they are likely to do next. Nearly all of the systems human beings have ever constructed for responding to each other are built on reading I Will / I Do and working backward toward conclusions about the interior the behavior originated from.

The conclusions are very often wrong. Simply because the task is structurally impossible. The interior is inaccessible. What is visible is the output. The space between them — the need that was pressing, the signal that was spinning, the ground that was present or absent, the story that was running — none of it is observable from the outside. It can only be inferred, and the inference is almost always contaminated by the observer's own bio-loop, their own stories, their own conclusions about what behavior means and what kind of person produces it.

The DSM is a catalog of I Will / I Do presentations. It describes, with considerable precision, the patterns of behavior and reported experience that tend to cluster together in ways that are clinically recognizable and practically useful. What it fails to do — what no outside observation can do — is locate the need. It can describe the output with great accuracy. It reliably fails to access the source. The diagnosis names the weather. It does not name what the bio-loop was reaching for when it produced that weather.

This is not a criticism of the people who built these systems or the people who work within them. They are doing what any observer can do: reading what is visible, working backward toward what is not. The limitation is not in the intelligence or the intention. It is structural. The observer will always be working with the output. Only the person navigating the storm in whom the bio-loop is spinning has access to the source.

An ill-conceived notion underlies much of how systems respond to difficult behavior: that identifying it precisely enough, classifying it, categorizing it — especially with the intent of punishing it — will somehow resolve the problem and eliminate the behavior. That reading the behavior accurately enough and labeling it or applying pressure externally will correct what the invisible pressures are generating.

It will not. It cannot. The bio-loop does not respond to the label the way the label maker intends. It responds to the need. The label itself becomes new input — registered as threat, as verdict, as one more signal the loop must now carry. And a system built entirely around reading and responding to the output, without access to the source, will keep producing what such systems have always produced — people who are somewhat more managed and no less lost.

The behavioral health field has built an extraordinary apparatus around human suffering. Diagnostic systems, therapeutic modalities, pharmacological interventions, treatment protocols — the accumulated effort of a century of clinical science. Much of it has helped. Some of it has saved lives.

The approaches that work best share a structural feature: they help the person access their own interior rather than assessing and adjusting from without. The therapist who creates enough safety for genuine signals to surface. The medication that quiets enough noise for the bio-loop's report to become audible. The group that receives the signal honestly enough that the person learns their signals mean something and can be brought into relationship without making the world more dangerous. The motivational interviewer who helps the person hear their own reasons rather than supplying reasons from outside.

These work because they are moving in the same direction as the Compass — toward the source rather than the output. They create the conditions under which inside-out navigation becomes possible.

The Compass is a reliable instrument for that same territory. It does not replace the clinical expertise, the containment, or the relational safety those approaches provide. It works alongside them — available in the gaps between sessions, in the moments outside every container, in the daily navigation that happens when no guide is present. A person in therapy who also holds the Compass has more access to what the therapy is trying to reach. A person on medication who can read their own bio-loop has better information about what the medication is doing and what it isn't.

The cursory treatment of that corpus in this chapter is not a verdict on its value. It is a reflection of starting position. The behavioral health field begins from the outside and works inward with great skill and genuine care. The Compass begins from the inside. The two are most useful when they work together.

The research that maps the mechanism most precisely comes from a different field entirely.

Daniel Kahneman, synthesizing decades of research on judgment and decision-making, identified two modes of mental operation. One is fast, automatic, effortless — the mode that reacts to threat before deliberation has begun, reaches for the familiar pattern, executes through what has worked before. The other is slow, considered, effortful — the mode that weighs options, overrides automatic responses, and holds the gap open long enough for choice to become possible. The Compass calls this second mode Deliberate Presence.

The territory Kahneman mapped is the same territory the Guide names. I Do is the automatic mode executing. The bio-loop responding to signal with the speed that kept the species alive when predators were the primary problem. I Will is Deliberate Presence available — the gap open, the slower processing engaged, the capacity to ask before the action expresses outward whether this is the intended direction. What Kahneman's research documented, and what the Guide names as compression, is the mechanism by which Deliberate Presence fatigues under load and the automatic mode takes over by default. The gap narrows not through moral failure but through resource depletion.

Antonio Damasio's research revealed the inverse. His patients with damage to emotional processing centers could analyze endlessly but could not decide. Without access to the body's signals — without I Feel informing the deliberation — Deliberate Presence spun without resolution. The somatic markers that normally guide choice toward one option and away from another were unavailable. The result was not irrationality but paralysis. I Will requires I Feel. Deliberate intention is not pure cognition operating above the body's noise. It is cognition informed by the body's signals, or it is cognition that cannot land.

The grammar of everyday speech has been pointing at this mechanism longer than the research has named it. *I feel this is the right thing to do. I don't feel I should. Trust your gut. My heart says.* These are not metaphors that drifted into common usage accidentally. They are the vernacular's honest report of what Damasio's patients lost — the body's signal informing deliberation before the conclusion has formed, guiding choice toward one option and away from another through a process that precedes and enables the slower reasoning.

The language knew before the research confirmed it.

Which makes the grammatical collapse the Guide identified in I Think more than a stylistic concern. *I am anxious* does not merely describe fusion with the signal. It performs it — installing the body's report as identity rather than information. *I feel anxious* preserves the distinction the vernacular has always tried to hold. The signal is present. The person receiving it is also present. Those are not the same thing.

I Will / I Do is where that distinction either holds or collapses in the world's view. The behavior expressed outward gets read, labeled, fed back. The language the world uses — and the language the person eventually uses about themselves — either names the output as output or installs it as character. The bio-loop receives both. It responds to both. The label that lands as verdict becomes part of the load the next action has to carry.

The Gap Made Habitable

The alternative to reading the output works from the inside out.

The Compass does not require the world to see the need. It requires only that the person whose bio-loop is spinning can see it. That the signal can be located before it escalates through the full cascade into behavior the world will read as character. That the need can be addressed at the source rather than managed at the output.

This is what changes when a person finds the Compass. The storm doesn't subside. The world's tendency to read the behavior and call it the person continues. The systems built around that reading still operate. What changes is the relationship between the bio-loop's interior and its expression. The slight but crucial gap — the breath-sized space — between the signal and the action, in which something that could be called choosing becomes possible.

I Will is that gap made habitable.

Imperfectly. Incompletely. As a bearing that holds rather than eliminates — that asks, in the middle of whatever is currently spinning: *is this what I actually intend?* Is this action — the one the bio-loop's pressing is about to express outward — the direction I am choosing to move?

Sometimes the answer is yes. The intention and the action are continuous. The person is home when the movement happens.

Sometimes the answer is no, or not quite, or not like this. And in that recognition, however small, something becomes possible that was not possible before. Not the elimination of the action. The capacity to pause before it. To ask what the bio-loop is actually signaling. To approach closer to the need. To bring the full sweep of the Compass to bear on what is about to happen before it happens.

I Do remains. Always. The bio-loop demands action — that is what being alive is. At the far end of the compression, when no other bearing is readable, I Do is still spinning. The action still happens. The bio-loop still expresses.

The Compass does not eliminate I Do. It makes I Will possible alongside it. The intention flowing into the action. The person present when the movement happens. The bio-loop expressing outward not just what the need was driving but what the person, having located the need, has chosen to do about it.

Five Sentences:

I Am — the ground from which the Compass is held.

I Think — the story the mind is telling.

I Feel — the signal the body is sending.

I Need — what the bio-loop is actually requiring.

I Will / I Do — the action that expresses outward, where the world finally sees what the interior has been spinning.

The bio-loop will keep spinning. The signal will keep reporting.

The instrument is now in your hand. The bearings are available. What the deliberate turn toward the signal makes legible, I Will / I Do carries into the world.

That is enough to begin.

Chapter 12 — The Sweep

It is a horizon read all at once, not in sequence. Locate. Differentiate. Inform action. When the sentences go quiet — use what remains. I Feel is almost always present. Start there.

I was sitting on the floor of a house where I no longer belonged, surrounded by boxes that felt like a burial. The divorce was final, the job was gone, and I was being evicted from the ground I was sitting on. It was two in the morning, and the story machine in my head had finally run out of explanations. It was just white noise — a high-frequency scream of *what now?* and *how could you?* and *it's over.*

In the corner of my mind, the old compulsion was calling. It wasn't a choice; it was a pull, as physical as gravity. The bio-loop was screaming for relief, for a way to turn down the volume of the storm, and it was reaching for the familiar proxy to provide temporary respite.

At that moment, I didn't have a plan. I didn't have willpower. I was below the functional threshold where those things live. I had only one sentence left: **I Feel.**

And the I Feel was a crushing, tectonic weight.

I performed what I now call **The Sweep**. I didn't know I was doing it. I didn't do it to feel better. I did it because I was a navigator who had lost the road, and I needed to know if I was still here. Still somehow relevant sitting alone in the dark.

I felt the floorboards beneath my legs. Cold. Hard. Indifferent. I recognized the ground — the simple, non-functional fact of my existence that was still there, even though the story of my life had collapsed. I was searching for **I Am.** Trying to inhabit the part of me that could observe the storm moving through me without becoming it.

I stayed with the weight in my chest. I didn't try to breathe it away. I just noticed it. *This is what I feel.* It was raw, unadorned grief, vibrating at a frequency that made my teeth ache. I had located **I Feel.** I stayed with it. I just let myself feel it.

I looked at the white noise in my head. It was racing now even faster because of allowing the feeling to express. I didn't argue with it. I was able to see it as a narration — the head-brain frantically assembling a catastrophe to match the signal the heart was sending. *The story is not the storm.* I was observing **I Think.**

After I was able to let the narration play out, without letting it lead me, not arguing with it, just letting it run, I felt myself settle just a fraction. From that space, I looked past the pull of the old compulsion. I searched for what I actually required. I didn't need the substance; I needed safety. I needed to be heard. I needed the weight to be acknowledged without being judged. I found **I Need.** What was present under the sensations.

I didn't promise to fix my life or commit to a five-year plan. I simply articulated the only action I could actually afford in that moment: *I will sit here until the sun comes up.* I intentionally performed **I Will / I Do.**

I wasn't "conditioning" myself for future success. I was simply reaching for orientation in a moment of maximum load. I was finding the coordinates of my own survival. I intentionally took the least damaging, most willful action I could find available.

When the sun finally hit the floorboards, the crisis wasn't gone. I was still sitting in a place I no longer belonged. I was still unemployed. The marriage was still over. But I was still sober. And I was no longer a ghost in my own storm. I had found the ground, and for the first time in months, I knew exactly where I was standing.

This is what the Compass does when we use it the way it was meant to be used.

The Five Sentences were meant to be held *during* the storm. The sweep is the Compass in motion — all five domains read at once, the way a navigator reads the entire horizon rather than scanning from left to right and waiting to reach east before looking south.

The sweep has three movements.

Locate. Where are you in the storm right now? What sentences are available? What has gone quiet?

If the storm is raging and you can't find anything else, you can start with the body. Breath is always present. When even I Feel is compressed, the breath can be the entry into what the bio-loop is signaling in the body. Notice the breath, whatever it is doing. Its rhythm, its rate, where it goes — into the chest, the belly. If it feels right, stay with it. If not, move on.

Physical sensation is also always present. You are always touching something. Notice that. The weight of your body pushing against the floor or the chair, the pressure against whatever is holding you. The temperature and texture of the air you are breathing, wherever you are. The consistency of anything your skin is touching. The tension in your face, your jaw, the shoulders, the gut, the hands. Not to relax, but to feel what is here, to notice it.

These are the rungs beneath I Feel. When even the feeling seems out of reach, they remain. The body is always reporting something.

From the body, the bearing becomes findable. On the floor that night, I started with what was physically present — the cold floorboards, the shallow breath, the locked jaw. From there I found the weight in my chest. From the weight, I found I Feel. That was the aperture. That was where navigation could begin.

Differentiate. What is the signal, and what is the story? What is the need, and what is the substitute? What is happening in the body, and what is happening in the narrative about the body?

The signal lives in the body. It arrives as sensation — weight, constriction, pressure, temperature, the physical textures you just located. It doesn't use words. It doesn't explain itself. It reports.

The story lives in language. It arrives as narration — *this is happening because, this means that, this is who I am, this is what comes next.* It assembles. It predicts. It builds rooms.

The signal and the story are not the same thing. They feel like the same thing because they arrive together, because the story was already playing out when the signal arrived. The story is always running. But they can be separated. The signal is what the body is carrying. The story is what the mind is constructing around it.

The need is what the bio-loop actually requires. The substitute is what the we reach for when the direct route feels unavailable. They point in the same direction. Only one closes the gap. But it requires a pause. A breath-sized space between the signal and the action. Without the pause the proxy appears without consideration and is reached for without hesitation.

On the floor that night, the white noise in my head was not the grief. The pull toward the old compulsion was not the need. The story machine was assembling a catastrophe. The bio-loop was signaling something simpler: I needed safety, needed to be heard, needed the weight acknowledged without judgment. The proxy would have quieted the noise. It would not have addressed the authentic signal that was generating it.

Inform action. Whatever the sweep finds, it feeds forward. Not as command. As the clearest available information about what the loop requires and what options remain open. On that floor, the information was: I need to be heard, need the weight acknowledged, need safety. The action available was minimal: sit here until the sun comes up. That was enough. That was what remained.

The sentences get lost under load. They diminish in a recognizable sequence.

I Think loses legibility first. The predictive, narrative mind doesn't always go quiet under pressure — it often gets louder. Sometimes dramatically. The story machine spins faster, generating noise so dense it becomes indecipherable. What collapses is not the volume but the coherence. When I Think has lost legibility, we cannot use the Compass to examine the story we are telling ourself, because the narrative has become white noise rather than something that can be observed as story. This is not a failure of the Compass. It is the Compass reporting accurately: the prediction mechanism is currently spinning out of control.

I Will goes next, or alongside. I Will requires Deliberate Presence — ground that high load cannot sustain. When I Will and I Do compress, and only I Do is present, we are still acting, still moving through our life. But the Deliberate Presence that I Will requires has nowhere to stand. The action is happening. The driver is operating on autopilot.

I Need dims when the bio-loop is pressing toward action without a legible signal about what it actually requires. This is among the more difficult navigational states — not because something has gone wrong with the person, but because the person is now moving without being able to accurately see what it is moving toward.

I Feel is the sentence that persists longest. Under any load we can survive, some version of the affective signal remains — compressed, perhaps, muted or distorted by the magnitude of the storm, but present. The valence is there. The body is still reporting.

And from that single sentence — from whatever remains when the rest has gone quiet — the sweep can begin.

You do not need all five to navigate. You use what is available.

The partial sweep, performed under conditions that permit only partial access, is complete navigation. It is navigation performed accurately under the conditions that actually exist.

The instrument responds to the state of the one using it. Under high load, it returns a partial reading. Under lower load, it returns more. This is not a flaw in the design. The instrument that reported clear signals regardless of the user's state would be lying. The bio-loop does not lie. The signals generated are genuine before they get misinterpreted or misdirected.

What the sweep offers is honesty about the present state, whatever that state is. And an honest reading — even a partial one, even a reading that says only *here is the feeling and here is the ground and I cannot currently find anything else* — that reading is the difference between moving through the storm blindly and moving through it with whatever sight the storm currently permits.

That is all it was ever promising.

That is enough.

— In Brief

The Five Sentences are a sweep — all five domains read at once, a horizon scan rather than a sequence.

Under load, I Think goes first. I Will follows. I Need can be invisible. I Feel persists longest. This is not failure; it is the Compass telling you where you are.

You don't need all five to navigate. Use what remains.

Locate: where are you right now? What is available?

Differentiate: what is signal and what is story? What is need and what is substitute?

Inform action: what the sweep finds feeds forward into the next available thing.

A partial sweep under high load is accurate navigation under the conditions that currently exist.

Use what remains.

Chapter 13 — In the Calm Before the Storm

The gap between I Will and I Do can be widened in advance. Not by trying harder. By building the structure that holds when trying harder is no longer available.

The Sweep showed what the Compass can do under load. This chapter asks something different: how to prepare for the storm before it arrives.

Deliberate Presence depletes. The gap between I Will and I Do closes. Trying harder is itself a Deliberate Presence operation — it requires the resource it is trying to replace. But the gap can be widened in advance, by building a structure that does not require Deliberate Presence to activate.

There is a woman we opened with in the Introduction.

She was sitting on her bed at 4 a.m. with the scenes from the previous day replaying in her head. The day at work she had barely endured. The court order he still hadn't complied with. The conversation with her daughter. The tone of her own voice when she said the thing she shouldn't have said.

The way her daughter looked at her before turning away.

She was painfully aware in that moment it could not be taken back, and the damage it caused would linger. She kept wondering why she had said it. She knew her daughter was too young to understand why her daddy had to leave them. She knew she needed to comfort, not scold.

But in that moment, when her daughter seemed to be testing her, it came without a thought. She heard the words coming out of her mouth before she realized they were hers.

That was then.

Some weeks later she meets a moment close enough to recognize.

The day has been the same kind of day. The bills are still due. The court order is still not complied with. She is still doing all of it alone. Her daughter says something in the tone daughters sometimes use — the tone that finds exactly the place that is already tender and applies exactly the pressure that place cannot currently hold.

She feels the sharp inhale. The turning toward. The lean. The finger that has not yet risen but is already preparing.

She has felt this before. Not in this moment — before this moment, in the calm of a Sunday afternoon when nothing was wrong and Deliberate Presence was available enough to notice the pattern and build something into it. She had learned to read these signals as the announcement that a response was already forming.

She came to recognize the feeling before she was taken over by it — the sharp inhale as she prepared to snap a response, the turning toward and leaning in with an urge to point a finger — these were her cues to access the preloaded link.

She had built one link. Simple. Physical. *If I feel the sharp inhale and the lean, then my first word is an exhale.*

The cue arrived. The link activated. The exhale came before the word did.

One breath is not very much.

It is also not nothing.

In that breath something became available that was not available the last time. Not calm. Not wisdom. The bio-loop was still under load and the day was still the same day. What became available was a bearing. One reading. I Think — the story loading in the back of the mind is not the whole truth of this child or this moment. I Feel — the tightness in the chest is real and it is older than this conversation.

The words that came were not perfect. The moment was not repaired. Her daughter did not suddenly understand what she was carrying or why the day had cost what it cost.

But the words were hers. She heard them coming out of her mouth and recognized them as chosen. Not performed from calm she didn't have. Chosen from the gap the exhale had opened — the gap the structure had built into the moment before the moment arrived.

That night at four in the morning the loop still ran. The bills were still due. The court order was still not complied with. She was still doing all of it alone.

But the conversation with her daughter was not on the list.

She had seen the storm as a storm instead of being swept away by it.

That is all the Compass has ever promised.

The structure that made the exhale possible was built before the moment arrived.

The form is simple: if X happens, then I will do Y. A link between a cue the body already announces and a response chosen in advance. When the cue arrives, the response initiates — not because she remembered, not because she had enough Deliberate Presence to choose in the moment, but because the link was already there waiting for the cue to activate it.

This is not a breathing technique. The exhale was hers — the specific, physical pause her body could execute when everything else had compressed. Someone else's gap might be a step taken, a hand opened, a window looked toward, a word said inward before the first word said outward. The gesture has to be found, not borrowed. A borrowed gesture carries the same load as remembering to use it. It fails at exactly the moment it is needed.

The cues are also personal. The sharp inhale, the lean, the urge toward the pointing finger — she found those by sitting with her own loop long enough in the calm to notice what the body announces just before the automatic response completes itself. That announcement is already there in every bio-loop. The calm is when it becomes audible.

Find the announcement. Build the link. Build it when Deliberate Presence is available — on a quiet afternoon, before the storm, not during it. The structure asks only that. What it returns is a gap that does not depend on Deliberate Presence to hold it open.

The Explored section develops the research behind why this works for the curious reader.

What you need to use it is already here.

— Explored

The gap between I Will and I Do is not a character flaw. It is a resource problem.

Daniel Kahneman spent decades mapping what happens to the deliberative system under demand. The capacity he identified — slow, considered, effortful, capable of holding the breath-sized space between impulse and action — is finite. It depletes through use. Under stress, cognitive load, the accumulated weight of a day or a life spent managing more than the system was designed to carry, that capacity stops being available. The faster, automatic system takes over by default. Not because it has been chosen. Because Deliberate Presence is no longer present to choose.

This is the mechanism the Guide calls compression. The gap narrows not through moral failure but through resource depletion. The ground is not absent. It is temporarily inaccessible. The bio-loop defaults to what is fastest and most available — the next available thing — because the slower, more deliberate processing has been outpaced by the conditions.

The problem this creates is precise: the gap is least available exactly when the cost of losing it is highest. Under light load, when the signal is quiet and the ground is stable, Deliberate Presence is easy to find. The gap holds open without effort. The bearing is readable. The person is home when the action happens.

Under heavy load — the day that asked too much, the relationship under strain, the old signal rising faster than the new awareness can meet it — Deliberate Presence is the first resource to go. The gap closes. The automatic system executes. The next available thing arrives before the question could be asked.

Trying harder does not solve this. Trying harder is itself a Deliberate Presence operation. It requires the resource it is trying to replace. Asking a depleted system to deliberate more is asking it to do the one thing it has lost the capacity to do. The effort increases pressure. The pressure accelerates depletion. The gap closes faster.

The Structure That Survives

Peter Gollwitzer spent decades studying a specific form of planning he called implementation intentions. The structure is simple: if X happens, then I will do Y. A link between a situational cue and a planned response. The research findings are not simple at all.

What implementation intentions appear to do — across hundreds of studies, across populations from healthy adults to people managing depression, chronic illness, addiction recovery, and goals that had previously resisted every conscious effort to pursue them — is delegate the initiation of action from the deliberative system to the automatic one. The if-then creates a link between a cue and a response. When the cue appears, the response initiates without requiring the slow, effortful processing that would otherwise be needed — and that might not be available under load.

The mechanism matters. The intention is not held in mind as something to remember. It is built into a structure that activates when the cue appears. When Deliberate Presence is available, the if-then is one path among many. When Deliberate Presence fatigues and the automatic system takes over, the if-then is one of the few paths that remains — because the automatic system, not the deliberative one, is what executes the response.

The collapse is leveraged.

Rather than fighting the fatigue — asking the depleted system to perform what it can no longer perform — the if-then uses the very mechanism that closes the gap to execute the response the gap would have produced. The automatic system, which takes over when Deliberate Presence depletes, is the same system that activates the pre-built link. The structure survives the conditions that defeat every other approach because it was designed for exactly those conditions.

The gap is not widened by holding it open under load. It is widened in advance by building a structure that does not require the gap to be held.

What This Is and Is Not

The structure works. This is not a motivational claim. It is a research finding replicated across populations, conditions, and goal domains for decades. The if-then structure reliably increases the probability that intention becomes action — not because it makes people more disciplined or more committed, but because it delegates initiation from a system that fatigues to a system that does not.

That distinction is the difference between a technique and a structure.

A technique requires the capacity to execute it. The breathing exercise that requires remembering to take control of the breath. The pause that requires remembering to pause. The reframe that requires the cognitive space to reframe. These are genuine tools and they genuinely help — when Deliberate Presence is available enough to reach for them. Under sufficient load, when Deliberate Presence has depleted past the threshold where reaching is possible, techniques are only as available as the capacity that was supposed to execute them.

Which is to say: not very.

The structure does not ask Deliberate Presence to reach for it in the moment. It was built into the moment before the moment arrived. When the cue appears the response initiates, simply because the link was established when capacity was present and no longer requires capacity to activate.

This is why structural understanding adapts where technique fails. The person who understands why the structure works can build links that fit their specific cues, their specific storms, their specific bio-loop's particular signals. When one link fails under load they can build a better one in the next available calm. When the storm produces a cue they had not anticipated they can recognize the structure well enough to improvise.

The person who has been given a technique without the structure underneath it has a tool that works in the conditions it was designed for and fails in the conditions it wasn't. They cannot adapt it because they do not know why it works. They can only repeat it and hope the conditions cooperate.

In the calm before the storm, build the tool designed to work in the storm, so when the storm is raging the right tool is already in your hand.

The Compass has always been structural rather than technical for exactly this reason. The Five Sentences are not steps to follow. They are a description of what is already happening in the bio-loop — made legible enough that the person navigating the storm can read what the storm is producing rather than being produced by it. The structure of this chapter extends that same principle one step further: not only can the storm be read, the conditions for reading it can be prepared in advance.

Not perfectly. Not always. Not as a guarantee that the gap will hold when the load is heaviest.

But reliably enough to make a difference.

The calm before the storm is not wasted time.

It is the only time the structure can be built.

— In Brief

The gap closes under load.

Trying harder closes it faster.

Build the structure before the storm arrives.

Find the cue — what the body announces just before the automatic response completes.

Something physical. Something yours.

Build the link: if that happens, then I will do this.

One link. Simple. Physical. Personal.

The link activates when Deliberate Presence cannot.

That is why it works.

Build it in the calm.

Not during the storm.

Use it.

Conclusion: The Convergence

Come back with me to the cliff walls. The fire is low. The circle is close. Outside, the night is everything the night has always been — indifferent, vast, full of sounds that do not organize themselves around human need or human comfort. Inside, something is being passed from one person to another. Not an object. An instrument. Something that works, that has always worked, that will be wrapped in whatever language the moment can sustain, and it is carried forward because it is too important to lose.

Every tradition that took the problem seriously enough to stay with it long enough found the same thing.

The Vedic priest chanting in the early morning. The Stoic examining his thoughts before dawn. The contemplative in silent prayer. The Sufi in ecstatic dissolution. The Zen practitioner sitting until the thinking mind exhausted itself. The person in a basement meeting room who said the true thing for the first time in a circle of people who knew it from the inside.

Different roads. Different centuries. Different languages and frameworks and assumptions about how the universe was organized.

The same instrument.

Not because they compared notes. Because the instrument was tracking something real — something that does not change across cultures or centuries because it is not cultural. Because it is biological. Because it is the structure of the bio-loop itself.

They did not have the biology to say why it worked. They knew something better — they knew it worked. They preserved it at enormous cost, wrapped it in whatever vessel the moment could sustain, transmitted it to whoever arrived at the edge of what the available instruments could reach.

Now we have the biology. The explanation does not diminish what they found. It honors it — and makes the instrument available without requiring any particular tradition or any particular metaphysical commitment.

This book is one more vessel. One more transmission.

What it carries is narrow. The Compass locates the signal. It reads the need. It names what the bio-loop requires. It makes a single life legible to the one living it. That is not a small thing. Most people live an entire life without their own loop ever being readable to themselves.

But this book has been about the one.

The one bio-loop spinning. The one person under load. The one reader holding the instrument, finding the ground, moving through the storm with whatever the conditions permit. Every chapter has assumed a single navigator doing this work alone with their own weather.

That assumption has been a simplification.

You do not live alone. You have never lived alone. The storms that have shaped you have been populated storms — by the people who were present and the people who were absent, by the loops that met yours and the loops that did not, by the reception offered and the reception withheld. The bio-loop spins in a single organism. It was never meant to resolve there.

The mattering signal does not close inside the one who generates it. It is a call written for two voices. The signal transmits. The phrase hangs open. What completes it is not the person's own effort but another person's presence — received accurately enough that the bio-loop can finally quiet what it has been carrying. The Compass, however well-read, cannot manufacture that reception. It can only locate the signal that is waiting for it.

Which means the solo Compass has a structural edge.

There are storms it can navigate. The 4 a.m. wakefulness. The conference room under load. The floor at 2 a.m. The pull of the proxy on a Tuesday. The instrument works in these conditions. If you have read this far, you have what you need to read your own loop through your own storms.

There are also storms the solo Compass locates but cannot close. The signal that requires reception to resolve. The need that is not for rest or safety or quiet but for contact — the specific ordering that happens in the body when another person has received what the loop has been transmitting. Not stillness. Coherence. The chaotic signal finding its integrated form. The way cream in coffee stops being two substances and becomes one system. The way a lake under turbulence smooths not into nothing but into surface. The loop does not quiet when received. It resolves.

The Compass reads that need accurately. What it cannot do is produce the ordering alone.

The mechanism does not stop at two. A group of people in genuine contact produces a coherence no individual among them could produce alone — which is why the containers existed, and why their loss matters. A clan around a fire. A meeting room. A congregation. A choir. The loops that found each other at that scale generated an ordering the individual cannot reach.

Beyond the group is the species. And beyond the species is the question of what the coherence itself is, and whether it points at something more than biological accident.

Those territories require their own instruments. This book is at the threshold between the one and the two.

What the solo Compass does, at this threshold, is change what is possible next. The person who can read their own loop can begin to read — imperfectly, partially, with care — what another person's loop might be signaling underneath their behavior. Not to fix it. Not to diagnose. Just to recognize that the other person is also a bio-loop, pressing toward what it requires, reading its own storm with whatever instrument it has or hasn't been given.

The recognition alone changes something. What changes is not the other person. What changes is the quality of presence you can bring to them.

That presence is the condition reception requires. It is also the condition the Compass makes possible.

Here is what the bio-loop does when the solo Compass is readable and the ground is present.

The signal received without being fused with. The need located beneath the substitution. The story seen as story rather than territory. The ground held through all of it. The full intelligence available to what comes next.

The spark finding the ground.

The ground beneath the storm — the simple, irreducible fact of being here, in this body, as the one to whom all of this is happening. I Am as the foundation that does not move when everything else is moving. But ground carries a second meaning: the electrical ground, the return path, the reference point without which the current has nowhere to flow and the circuit cannot complete. I Am is the ground in both senses simultaneously. The foundation you stand on. The pole the spark must find for the current to move.

And I Feel is the spark finding it.

The signal that proves we are alive. The biological evidence of existence. The correction to Descartes that the body has been offering since before philosophy had language for it. *I feel, therefore I am* — not as a refinement of the old claim but as the completion of it. The spark and the ground meeting. The circuit closing. The current flowing through the full sweep of the Compass, bearing by bearing, the bio-loop finally doing what it always presses toward.

Constantly signaling in an attempt to complete the circuit.

The bio-loop is always spinning. The ground is always present beneath the storm. The circuit is always available to complete whenever the spark and the ground are allowed to meet.

What was missing was not the capacity. What was missing was a way to locate what the capacity was doing.

Now you have it.

The storm is still outside. It always will be. The weather of being alive does not clear because the Compass is found — it remains what it has always been, the ongoing condition of a bio-loop navigating a world that was not designed to meet its needs perfectly or continuously or without cost.

But you know what you are standing on. You know how to find it when the storm makes it hard to feel. You know how to prepare in the calm before the storm grows. You know the signal is not the self. The story is not the territory. The need is real and has an address. The feeling is the proof of being alive and the most direct access to what the bio-loop is trying to say.

You know the bio-loop is never wrong. It is always faithful. Always signaling something real, through every channel it tries — waiting for the moment when something turns toward it and lets it be heard.

You know what the elders had that the woman at 4 a.m. does not. The pause. The culturally protected time in which the signal can arrive before the noise returns. The pause that modern life has eliminated, and that — when it does briefly remain — gets filled before it can become audible. You know the Compass works best in the gap that absence creates.

You know you are not alone in the storm. You have never been alone in it. The specific weight is yours — unrepeatable, particular, belonging entirely to the life you are living. The fact of the weight is older than your life and larger than your story, and is shared with every person who has a bio-loop spinning in difficult weather.

And when two storms meet — when the weather is shared intimately with another — the storms change form. They intensify. Whether that intensity becomes more navigable or more destructive depends significantly on what each person is carrying and how well they can read it. That territory deserves more than this book can give it.

There are storms so large, so pervasive, that a Compass alone cannot accommodate them. That territory requires a different instrument entirely. Those are subjects for other books.

The Compass is in your hands.

The ground is beneath your feet.

The signal is still pointing.

The circuit is available to complete.

You have everything you need to begin being less lost.

The Five Sentences — Reference Card

The Compass. Five Sentences. Incomplete. Use what is available. Curiosity Provides Access.

I Am The Compass's True North: the ground beneath the storm that makes the other bearings readable. Find it. Return to it. Find it again.

I Think The story the mind is telling right now. Let it finish. Notice that it is a story. Sit in the pause long enough for the right question to arrive. Ask it only when there is enough ground to ask honestly

I Feel The signal the body is sending right now, continually. Turn toward it. Let it be signal before it becomes explanation. Ask not *how* — ask *what.*

.**I Need** What the bio-loop is actually requiring beneath the signal and story. Not the substitute or the proxy. Let it show itself before naming it. Plainly, if you can.

I Will / I Do The only bearing anyone else can see. I Will — intention present. I Do — bio-loop executing. The gap between them is not failure. It is information.

The Sweep It is a horizon read all at once not in sequence. Locate. Differentiate. Inform action. When the sentences go quiet, I Feel is almost always present. Start there.

In the Calm The gap between I Will and I Do can be widened by building the structure in advance that holds when trying harder is no longer available.

The Conditions — Reference Card

What the Compass Requires. Incomplete. Use What is Available.

I Am — The Compass's True North: the ground beneath the storm that makes the other bearings readable. Find it. Return to it. Find it again.

Bio-Loop — In its simplest form: need, signal, action. In humans, the loop is shaped by body, belonging, narrative, meaning, and time. The Compass helps make its signals more legible.

Mind — named by function rather than essence: the mediating layer where body signal, story closure, and the deeper orientation toward what is actually present become distinguishable enough for navigation. Holds the Compass.

Attention — the faculty the mind wields. Its utility affects which signals the mind receives and their valence. Adjustable aperture and focus. It does not directly affect the bio-loop. It is used to read the bio-loop.

Curiosity — its orientation enables attention without coercion. Allows the mind to turn toward the bio-loop. instead of managing it. Provides engagement without fear so the Compass can be held without effort.

Time — accessible through patience. Signals must be allowed to surface at their own pace. The only truly limited resource. Use it wisely. Required for the Compass to read the signals of the bio-loop honestly.

In the Calm — build what holds the gap open in the storm.

You are not the storm. You are the one standing in it. That is enough to begin.

The Briefs — In Brief

The Bio-Loop — In Brief

The bio-loop is always spinning.

A need arises. A signal is sent. Action follows.

When the action meets the need the signal quiets. When it doesn't, the signal continues — often with more insistence.

More insistence brings more noise.

As humans we call that signal feeling. The feeling is the bio-loop doing its job. Signaling that something requires attention.

The storm is the weather of being alive. The bio loop is our answer to it — signaling what survival requires.

The Compass doesn't stop the storm. It points to the signals the bio-loop is sending within it.

That is enough for navigation.

The Mind — In Brief

Mind is named here by function. It is the mediating layer where body signal, story, attention, and action become distinguishable.

Most of the time, mind runs on automatic. Thoughts arrive. Stories generate. The narrative continues. This is the default pattern.

Deliberate Presence renders the Compass more readable: the capacity to notice what is happening without becoming fused with it.

Attention is the mind's aperture: whatever it turns toward becomes foreground.

Curiosity keeps the aperture open. The willingness to stay turned toward what is present before the story closes.

Curiosity is capacity-dependent. Under enough load, we reach for closure. When curiosity is available, the Compass becomes easier to read.

Mind holds the Compass. Attention turns it. Curiosity keeps it open. Legibility makes navigation possible.

Gut, Heart, Head — In Brief

The embodied signal centers. Each sends real information into the bio-loop.

Gut tends toward body-level need: the pressure of requirement before it has a name.

Heart tends toward felt state: the organism's affective report of how things are going.

The head-brain tends toward story: narrative, prediction, explanation, and meaning.

The story arrives quickly. Often it replaces the signal it was built from.

Attention can travel beneath the explanation. When it does, the signal becomes more readable.

The Compass is calibrated for the organism: gut, heart, head, ground, and action;

Need, Feel, Think, I Am, I Will / I Do.

I Am — In Brief

I Am is the Compass's True North: the ground beneath the storm.

You are aware that you exist.

That presence — the one noticing the weather, holding the Compass — is the ground.

It was here before this storm.

It will be here after.

Find it.

Return to it.

Find it again.

I Think — In Brief

The head-brain tells stories. It has to.

I Think is the bearing that notices the story has arrived.

When the story becomes visible, the pause opens.

In that pause, the right question can rise.

Is this true?

What has this story been protecting?

Was this story handed to me before I knew it was a story?

What need has been hidden underneath it?

Notice the story first.

The questions come after.

That is often enough to keep I Am from being occupied by the room the story built.

I Feel — In Brief

You are feeling something right now.

Maybe it is clear. Maybe it is vague. Maybe it has been quiet so long you stopped noticing it was there. Either way, the body is signaling.

I Feel is a turn toward that signal.

Notice what is here before deciding what it means or what to do about it.

Ask what is here. Not how do I feel. What the body is carrying right now.

Tightness. Weight. Warmth. Hollowness. Pressure.

The signal before its name.

Let the signal be a signal before it becomes a named explanation.

Notice it honestly if you can.

Then let the right question be asked.

I Need — In Brief

Before the story. Before the feeling.

The need was there first.

It is the source of the signal. The reason the bio-loop keeps moving at all. And it is the hardest part to see.

The substitute doesn't close the gap.

I Need is the bearing that looks underneath for the actual requirement.

Sometimes it arrives plainly. I need rest. I need help. I need to be seen. I need to be safe. Plain. Simple. True.

You do not have to know yet how the need will be met. Notice it first.

A need that has been noticed is different from a need that is still driving everything from underground.

A noticed need has an address.

And what has an address can eventually be found.

I Will / I Do — In Brief

This is the bearing the world sees.

Everything else — story, feeling, need — happens inside. What becomes visible is action. What you say. What you do. How you move.

I Will is intention present. The gap between impulse and movement open enough for choosing to stand there.

I Do is the bio-loop executing. Action without that gap. Not absence. Compression.

Most of life is lived between those ends. The distance is not moral. It is load.

The gap can widen. Needs addressed closer to the source. Signal quieter. Ground less compressed. More breath between the signal and the action.

Not control. Deliberate Presence. The person home when the action happens.

The Sweep — In Brief

The Five Sentences are a sweep — all five domains read at once, a horizon scan rather than a sequence.

Under load, I Think goes first. I Will follows. I Need can be invisible. I Feel persists longest. This is not failure; it is the Compass telling you where you are.

You don't need all five to navigate. Use what remains.

Locate: where are you right now? What is available?

Differentiate: what is signal and what is story? What is need and what is substitute?

Inform action: what the sweep finds feeds forward into the next available thing.

A partial sweep under high load is accurate navigation under the conditions that currently exist.

Use what remains.

In the Calm Before the Storm — In Brief

The gap closes under load.

Trying harder closes it faster.

Build the structure before the storm arrives.

Find the cue — what the body announces just before the automatic response completes.

Something physical. Something yours.

Build the link: if that happens, then I will do this.

One link. Simple. Physical. Personal.

The link activates when Deliberate Presence cannot.

That is why it works.

Build it in the calm.

Not during the storm.

Use it.

Together — In Brief

The Compass works in solitude. The bearings are available. The ground can be found alone.

But the bio-loop regulates optimally in relationship. The signal changes when it is genuinely received by another person. Not managed. Not performed. Received.

Two storms meeting without Compasses tend to become one larger storm. Each bio-loop reads the other's signal as threat. The reaching that finds a wall produces more signal, more defense, more distance.

Two storms meeting with Compasses can navigate together. One person finding ground. Seeing the other bio-loop — not the behavior, but what is underneath it. Offering that seeing without requiring the other to be different first.

Not fixed. Held.

In the holding, the next thing becomes possible.

Bibliography

Why We Are Not Lost

Wayne G. Williams

The works listed here are the ones this book names — the thinkers and researchers whose work appears in the text directly, and whose contributions are engaged in the argument. They are organized loosely by where they appear in the book's arc. The fuller scholarly apparatus — the wider research literature that shaped the thinking, the clinical work behind the framework, the deeper warrant for the claims the book makes — will be available at: https://waynegwilliams.com/

The Biology of the Loop

Bateson, Gregory. *Steps to an Ecology of Mind.* Chicago: University of Chicago Press, 1972.

The source of the bio-loop's conceptual backbone. Bateson documented feedback structures operating at every level of biological organization — information flowing between organism and environment, correcting course, maintaining viability. The book's central architecture is not borrowed from Bateson as metaphor. It is the same structure he identified already running in everything alive. He gave it a language precise enough to work with.

Cacioppo, John T., and William Patrick. *Loneliness: Human Nature and the Need for Social Connection.* New York: Norton, 2008.

Cacioppo spent decades demonstrating that social isolation is not merely unpleasant but physiologically threatening — elevating cortisol, disrupting sleep, accelerating cognitive decline, increasing mortality at rates comparable to smoking. The book's claim that belonging is a biological need, not a cultural preference, rests on this research. The bio-loop does not distinguish between the threat of a predator and the threat of exclusion from the group.

Frankl, Viktor E. *Man's Search for Meaning.* Translated by Ilse Lasch. Boston: Beacon Press, 1959.

Written from inside the concentration camps, Frankl documented what no controlled study could ethically produce: direct observation of what happens to the organism when meaning collapses entirely. His conclusion — that the will to meaning is a primary biological drive, as fundamental as hunger and as consequential when unmet — grounds the book's treatment of meaning as a need the bio-loop signals, not a luxury that arrives after other needs are secured.

Lakoff, George, and Mark Johnson. *Philosophy in the Flesh: The Embodied Mind and Its Challenge to Western Thought.* New York: Basic Books, 1999.

The argument that even the most abstract human concepts — meaning, purpose, belonging, the future — trace back through layers of embodied metaphor to the felt reality of being a body in the world. This is why the signal for meaning unmet and the signal for hunger unmet can feel, in the body, so similar. The bio-loop does not sort needs by the categories the mind uses. It registers gap. It generates signal.

Gershon, Michael D. *The Second Brain.* New York: Harper, 1998.

Gershon documented what the anatomy demonstrates: the gut's enteric nervous system operates with considerable independence from the head-brain, coordinating the internal environment and sending information upward through multiple channels simultaneously. The phrase "second brain" can be overstated. What it points toward cannot. It is what the book describes in the chapter on Gut, Heart, and Head.

Maslow, Abraham H. *Motivation and Personality.* New York: Harper & Row, 1954.

The hierarchy of needs — survival, safety, belonging, esteem, self-actualization — is one of the most influential frameworks ever applied to human motivation. The book engages it directly, and argues that the pyramid misrepresents how the bio-loop actually works. Needs do not resolve in sequence. They run in parallel, press simultaneously, and cannot be ranked out of their biological entanglement. Maslow found something real. The architecture he built around it has cost people the ability to take their own higher-order needs seriously.

The Mind and Its Stories

Wittgenstein, Ludwig. *Tractatus Logico-Philosophicus.* Translated by D.F. Pears and B.F. McGuinness. London: Routledge, 1961. *Philosophical Investigations.* Translated by G.E.M. Anscombe. Oxford: Blackwell, 1953.

Two works, one argument across two phases of thinking. From the *Tractatus*: the limits of my language are the limits of my world — the claim that grammar is not neutral, that the structure of a sentence helps constitute what can be seen, thought, and acted on. From the *Investigations*: the treatment of language as a form of life, in which the sentences we use are not merely describing the worlds we inhabit but participating in constructing them. Together, they are the philosophical ground for why *I am anxious* and *I feel anxious* are not stylistic variants. One performs the collapse it describes. The other preserves a distinction that makes navigation possible.

James, William. *The Principles of Psychology.* 2 vols. New York: Henry Holt, 1890.

The source of the distinction between the "I" and the "me" — the self as knower and the self as known — that grounds the book's treatment of I Am. The "me" is everything that can be made into an object of reflection: body, history, story, roles. The "I" is the one doing the reflecting. What James observed, and what the book builds on, is that the one looking never quite becomes an object in the same way. It is always there in the looking, always prior to what is being looked at.

Husserl, Edmund. *Ideas: General Introduction to Pure Phenomenology.* Translated by W.R. Boyce Gibson. London: Allen & Unwin, 1931.

The source of the epoché — the deliberate bracketing of assumptions about the external world so that experience itself can be examined more carefully. When Husserl looked there, he found that experience always has a basic shape: something is experienced, and something experiences it. The one to whom experience appears is always prior to what appears. The book uses this observation in the I Am chapter as one of several traditions that arrived at the same threshold from different directions.

Friston, Karl. "The Free-Energy Principle: A Unified Brain Theory?" *Nature Reviews Neuroscience* 11, no. 2 (2010): 127–138.

The theoretical foundation for understanding the brain as a prediction machine — an organ in the business of reducing uncertainty by generating models of the world and updating them only when evidence demands revision. What we experience as perception is not the raw feed from the senses. It is the brain's best guess, corrected at points of prediction error. The book's treatment of I Think as the story machine's continuous operation, running ahead of the signal, draws directly on Friston's framework.

Raichle, Marcus E. "The Brain's Default Mode Network." *Annual Review of Neuroscience* 38 (2015): 433–447.

The discovery that the so-called resting brain is not resting. Between tasks, a network remains continuously active — reviewing the past, modeling the future, maintaining the thread of self across time. The book's account of the mind as a narrative machine that runs stories before the signal has arrived, and keeps running them after, draws on what Raichle's research made visible about how the brain operates when attention is not captured from outside.

McEwen, Bruce S. "Stress, Adaptation, and Disease: Allostasis and Allostatic Load." *Annals of the New York Academy of Sciences* 840 (1998): 33–44.

The research distinguishing acute stress — the single demand the system was designed to meet and discharge — from accumulated load, which is what happens when demands arrive faster than the organism can metabolize them and the baseline itself shifts upward. The book's account of why the storm gets harder to navigate over time, and why the Compass is more difficult to read under chronic conditions than under acute ones, draws on McEwen's framework.

Descartes, René. *Meditations on First Philosophy.* 1641.

Descartes appears in this book not as a guide but as the position being corrected. His famous formulation — *I think, therefore I am* — located certainty in the most fragile and conditionally available of the Compass bearings, the first to go under load. The book's argument is that the body has been offering a more basic correction for as long as human beings have had bodies: *I feel, therefore I am.* Aliveness is evidenced not by thought, which requires conditions, but by signal, which continues when everything else has gone quiet.

The Compass and Its Bearings

Seligman, Martin E.P. *Helplessness: On Depression, Development, and Death.* San Francisco: W.H. Freeman, 1975.

The research establishing learned helplessness as a mechanism — organisms repeatedly exposed to conditions they cannot change stop attempting responses that might later become available, even when conditions change. The learning generalizes. The book's account of depression as the foreclosure of actionability — the bio-loop still signaling while the organism has stopped believing the signal points at anything addressable — draws on Seligman's documentation of how that foreclosure spreads and holds.

Hayes, Steven C., Kirk D. Strosahl, and Kelly G. Wilson. *Acceptance and Commitment Therapy: An Experiential Approach to Behavior Change.* New York: Guilford Press, 1999.

The clinical framework built around the distinction between fusion and defusion — the difference between *I am unlovable* and *I am having the thought that I am unlovable.* The book's treatment of I Think as a bearing that involves seeing the story as a story, rather than arguing with its content, draws directly on

Hayes's work. The content of the thought stays identical. The relationship to it shifts. And that shift changes what becomes possible next.

Damasio, Antonio. *Descartes' Error: Emotion, Reason, and the Human Brain.* New York: Putnam, 1994.

Damasio's patients with damage to emotional processing centers could analyze endlessly and arrive nowhere. Reasoning remained analytically intact while decision collapsed. Without the body's signals to mark what matters, the mind can compare, list, and weigh without being able to choose. The book's treatment of I Feel as foundational to I Will — that deliberate intention is not pure cognition but cognition informed by the body's signal, or cognition that cannot land — rests on Damasio's research.

Deci, Edward L., and Richard M. Ryan. "The 'What' and 'Why' of Goal Pursuits: Human Needs and the Self-Determination of Behavior." *Psychological Inquiry* 11, no. 4 (2000): 227–268.

Four decades of research identifying three psychological needs — autonomy, competence, and relatedness — that appear universally present across cultures, developmental stages, and human circumstance. The book's account of what the bio-loop is reaching toward in I Need draws on Deci and Ryan's framework as empirical warrant for the claim that certain needs are structural requirements, not preferences, and that their chronic frustration produces recognizable and predictable forms of suffering.

Maté, Gabor. *In the Realm of Hungry Ghosts: Close Encounters with Addiction.* Berkeley: North Atlantic Books, 2010.

Maté's central question — not what is wrong with you but why the pain? — runs beneath the book's entire account of substitution. The behavior makes sense once you can see what it is medicating. The need is always legitimate. The channel is what varies. Maté understood this more clearly than most, and with more compassion for the people caught inside it than the clinical literature has typically managed.

Kahneman, Daniel. *Thinking, Fast and Slow.* New York: Farrar, Straus and Giroux, 2011.

Decades of research on two modes of mental operation: fast and automatic versus slow, deliberate, and effortful. The book calls the latter Deliberate Presence. What Kahneman documented — and what Chapters 11 and 12 are built around — is the mechanism by which Deliberate Presence depletes under load and the automatic system takes over by default. Not through failure of character. Through resource exhaustion. The gap closes because it cannot be held, not because the person stopped trying.

Gollwitzer, Peter M. "Implementation Intentions: Strong Effects of Simple Plans." *American Psychologist* 54, no. 7 (1999): 493–503.

The research establishing that a specific structure of planning — if X happens, then I will do Y — reliably increases the probability that intention becomes action across a wide range of populations and conditions, including people managing depression, chronic illness, and goals that had resisted every previous effort. The insight at the center of Chapter 12: the if-then link delegates initiation from the deliberate system to the automatic one. It survives the conditions that defeat every other approach because it was built for exactly those conditions.

American Psychiatric Association. *Diagnostic and Statistical Manual of Mental Disorders,* 5th ed. Washington, DC: American Psychiatric Association, 2013.

The DSM appears in this book as an instrument to be understood rather than a text to be studied. The argument is not that it is wrong. It is that it is a symptom catalog — describing, with considerable precision, the patterns of behavior and reported experience that cluster in clinically recognizable ways, while reliably failing to access what the bio-loop was reaching for when it produced those patterns. The diagnosis names the weather. It does not locate what generated it.

Alcoholics Anonymous: The Story of How Many Thousands of Men and Women Have Recovered from Alcoholism. 4th ed. New York: Alcoholics Anonymous World Services, 2001.

The recovery rooms found something many clinical approaches have never reproduced at scale: the bio-loop carries its signal differently when the signal is no longer borne alone. People sat in a circle, told the truth, and were received by people who knew it from the inside — not as diagnosis, not as case, but as recognition. That discovery is real and has kept people alive who would not otherwise have survived. The book's critique of the *I am an addict* formulation is offered in full respect for what the rooms found. The grammar can be truer. The discovery stands.

A note on what is not listed here

The bibliography above is honest in a way the earlier version of this book was not: it names only what the book actually names. But honesty requires a second half.

What was cut from this book was not peripheral. It was formative — research and clinical work and ancient tradition that shaped every chapter, even the ones that never cite it directly. It was removed not because it was wrong or unimportant but because including it fully would have produced a different book: one defending its own scaffolding instead of serving the person holding it.

The clinical innovations are the most significant omission. Bessel van der Kolk's work on how traumatic experience is stored in the body rather than in explicit memory — the research that demonstrated, with clinical precision, why the body remains the bio-loop's fallback messenger long after language has explained the experience away. Peter Levine's development of Somatic Experiencing, and the decades of clinical work that demonstrated the body's own capacity to complete what overwhelming experience interrupted. Richard Schwartz's Internal Family Systems, which found the ground — the Self beneath the parts — and built a clinical container for working with it that the Compass, operating without a trained guide, can only approximate. Francine Shapiro's EMDR, and the structural insight the book wanted to explore but couldn't hold: that accessing one bearing by occupying another is not an accident but an architecture. William Miller and Stephen Rollnick's work on motivational interviewing, which demonstrated that the will to change cannot be installed from outside — that self-generated language about one's own reasons carries a weight that external argument cannot replicate. Judith Herman's account of complex trauma, and what her framework reveals about why the bio-loop builds the defenses it builds: not as malfunction, but as the intelligence of an organism that had no other option.

The developmental and relational science runs just as deep. John Bowlby's attachment theory, and Mary Ainsworth's observational extension of it, which together explain why some adults cannot locate what they need: they are still running the adaptive architecture of a child whose earliest signals were not reliably received. Stephen Porges's polyvagal framework, which gives neurological specificity to what the book can only gesture at — the autonomic hierarchy, the social nervous system, the body's continuous reading of safety and threat before the mind has formed a thought about it. Daniel Siegel's interpersonal neurobiology, and the clinical and developmental account of how one regulated nervous system shapes another. René Spitz's early research on infants in foundling homes, which remains the starkest available evidence that belonging is not a preference but a survival requirement — documented in the most unflinching terms the clinical literature has produced. Vincent Felitti's ACE studies, which measured the accumulated cost of a bio-loop that learned, early, that its signals would not be received, and traced that cost forward through a lifetime of outcomes that are still being reckoned with.

The ancient traditions were always in this book beneath the surface. The Stoic practice — Marcus Aurelius and Epictetus — as the clearest practical antecedent for what the Compass does: not the control of experience but the orientation within it, maintained through deliberate examination across decades of genuine difficulty. The Vedic traditions and the Upanishads, which approached the territory of I Am with a philosophical precision that Western psychology is still catching up to. The Buddhist account of awareness — luminous, ungraspable, the open field in which experience arises without being owned by it. The Sufi and Christian contemplative lineages, each arriving at the same structural threshold from a different direction, finding the ground without being able to name it in ways that would survive translation. Eugene Gendlin's Focusing, which gave Western clinical practice its most careful account of the felt sense — the pre-verbal, pre-conceptual knowing the body carries before words arrive for it — and documented, across decades of research, what actually produced change in human beings in genuine difficulty.

The physiological and neuroscientific warrant for the book's biological claims runs deeper than what appears in the text. Robert Sapolsky's decades of research on the stress response and its consequences when a system built for acute demands runs chronically. The HeartMath Institute's documentation of cardiac coherence and the heart's electromagnetic field — frontier material, bracketed carefully, but real enough that excluding it felt like a debt worth naming. Emeran Mayer's synthesis of the gut-brain axis, extending Gershon's foundational work into the full bidirectional complexity of what the microbiome contributes to mood, motivation, and the organism's baseline sense of what is possible.

The speech act theory — J.L. Austin's distinction between describing a state and constituting one, John Searle's elaboration of what makes a speech act perform what it claims to perform — was the philosophical backbone of the book's argument that the Five Sentences are navigation acts rather than descriptions. It was cut because the argument works without it. It was cut with some grief.

All of it is available. The full accounts, the clinical literature, the warrant for every claim the book makes but does not fully defend, the ancient texts that arrived at the same instrument centuries before the biology had language for why it worked — that is what the landing page is for.

What the book could offer was one thing done well: an instrument small enough to hold in the dark. What shaped that instrument is a much larger story. It is waiting for you when you are ready for it.

https://waynegwilliams.com/

The Compass points. The bibliography marks some of the roads that led to it.

www.ingramcontent.com/pod-product-compliance
Lightning Source LLC
LaVergne TN
LVHW100523110826
845146LV00002B/749

* 9 7 9 8 2 3 4 0 7 6 6 6 3 *